"Andy Stanley touches the right nerve at the right time. We all have an understandable tendency to focus on the problems *others* need to address in *their* lives. But Andy encourages us to put *ourselves* on the hook and not let go until we've made any necessary changes. *It Came from Within!* shined a spotlight on some of those areas I need to work on, and I know it will do the same for you."

—SHAUNTI FELDHAHN
Bestselling author of *For Women Only*

"Andy Stanley is a master teacher for a generation that loves to be taught. *It Came from Within!* is yet more proof of Andy's ability to take us deep in a way that makes us want to go there. This is a great book."

—DAVE RAMSEY
New York Times bestselling author
and nationally syndicated radio host

"Read this book with caution! You will probably uncover some mean and ugly stuff in the depths of your own heart. I sure did. The good news is that Andy Stanley doesn't leave you there to struggle; instead, he offers wise, biblical remedies that every Christian should make part of their own spiritual habits. This is great stuff that I enjoyed teaching at our church."

—DOUG FIELDS
Associate pastor, Saddleback Church

IT CAME FROM WITHIN!

IT CAME FROM WITHIN!

ANDY STANLEY

Multnomah Publishers® *Sisters, Oregon*

IT CAME FROM WITHIN!

published by Multnomah Publishers, Inc.

© 2006 by Andy Stanley

International Standard Book Number: 1-59052-510-8

Cover design by The DesignWorks Group Inc.
Cover image by Steve Bronstein/Getty Images
Interior design and typeset by Katherine Lloyd, The DESK

The author gratefully acknowledges ESPN.com and Wikipedia.org
as sources for the story and statistics of "Pistol Pete" Maravich.

Unless otherwise indicated, Scripture quotations are from:
The Holy Bible, New International Version © 1973, 1984 by International Bible Society,
used by permission of Zondervan Publishing House.

Other Scripture quotations are from:
New American Standard Bible® (NASB) © 1960, 1977, 1995
by the Lockman Foundation. Used by permission.
The Holy Bible, New King James Version (NKJV) © 1984 by Thomas Nelson, Inc.
The Holy Bible, King James Version (KJV)
The Holy Bible, English Standard Version (ESV) © 2001 by Crossway Bibles,
a division of Good News Publishers. Used by permission. All rights reserved.

Multnomah is a trademark of Multnomah Publishers, Inc.,
and is registered in the U.S. Patent and Trademark Office.
The colophon is a trademark of Multnomah Publishers, Inc.

Printed in the United States of America

For information:
MULTNOMAH PUBLISHERS, INC.
601 N LARCH STREET • SISTERS, OREGON 97759

Library of Congress Cataloging-in-Publication Data
Stanley, Andy.
It came from within! / Andy Stanley.
  p. cm.
ISBN 1-59052-510-8
1. Anger--Religious aspects--Christianity. 2. Avarice--Religious aspects--Christianity.
3. Guilt--Religious aspects--Christianity. 4. Jealousy--Religious aspects--Christianity.
I. Title.
BV4627.A5S73 2006
248.4--dc22
                                                              2005027126
06 07 08 09 10 11—10 9 8 7 6 5 4 3 2 1 0

Coming Attractions

PART IV
WE HAVEN'T SEEN THE LAST OF THEM

Acknowledgments

Publishing is never a solo effort. Behind every book there is a team of people whose talents and efforts make the author appear far better than he or she really is. So let me begin by thanking Don Jacobson for the opportunity to work with Multnomah Publishers. Don, what started as a business relationship has become a cherished friendship. Sandra and I are constantly telling people that you are one of the finest men we know.

Credit for the creative concept behind this book goes to my editor, David Webb. David, thanks for your patience, diligence, and unfiltered feedback.

I also want to say thanks to my mentor and friend Steve Yungerberg. Steve, thank you for more breakfast meetings than I can remember. Thank you for listening. Thank you for driving across town to assure me that I was going to be fine. Your insights were life changing. You were there for me in my darkest hours. I could never say thank you enough. My hope is that this book will in some small way do for others what you did for me. Thank you.

Sneak Preview

Cora: *We're going to see things no one has ever seen before. Just think about it.*

Grant: *That's the trouble. I am.*

FANTASTIC VOYAGE (1966)

Newt: *My mommy always said there were no monsters—no real ones. But there are, aren't there?*

Ripley: *Yes, there are.*

Newt: *Why do they tell little kids that?*

Ripley: *Most of the time it's true.*

ALIENS (1986)

I'm sure you will agree that the 1986 sci-fi thriller *Aliens* is one of the finest films ever released. It's got everything. A brilliant plot. Great acting. Drama. Love. And an ending that sucks the breath right out of you. It's one of those movies you want to see again and again. Everybody loves *Aliens*.

Don't they?

You say you've never seen it?

You saw it and hated it?

Your parents wouldn't even let you see it?

Okay, maybe everybody doesn't share my enthusiasm for the classics, but it really is a great movie. In fact, *Aliens* is the ultimate "chick flick." The main character is a woman intent on rescuing a little girl from a female alien, who is equally intent on using the little girl as a host for her eggs. It's a relationship movie from start to finish.

In the closing moments of the film, Ellen Ripley (played by Sigourney Weaver) tucks Newt, the rescued girl, into bed as they prepare for their long flight back to earth. In their final exchange Newt asks, "Can I dream?"

"Yes, honey," Ripley replies, "I think we both can. Sleep tight."

It doesn't get any better than that.

I'm getting misty just thinking about it.

PLAYING HOST

Just in case you haven't actually seen the movie, let me give you a quick overview. The plot revolves around the mysterious disappearance of an entire colony of people living and working on the planet LV-426. When the company sponsoring the work on LV-426 are unable to reestablish contact with the colonists, they call in the marines. Upon arrival, the elite squad of space marines are confronted with a grisly situation: The colonists have been taken alive by extraterrestrial creatures—aliens—to serve as hosts for their embryos. Once the embryo is implanted in a living host—in this case, the colonist—the individual is able to function normally for a while. But when the gestation process is complete, the infant alien bursts out through the midsection of the host, killing him or her in the process.

Fortunately for the marines, Ellen Ripley has encountered this species before and is brought along as an observer. Early in the film, when the marines find themselves overmatched, Ripley assumes command and suggests that they nuke the entire planet. In her words, "It's the only way to be sure." As Hollywood would have it, however, things don't go exactly as planned. The aliens prove to be far more intelligent and extraordinarily more resilient than Ripley and her space warriors first anticipate. The movie culminates in a one-on-one confrontation between Ripley and the alien queen. In the end, Ripley prevails—but only to the point of leaving the door open for two sequels.

MOMMY WAS WRONG

As unrealistic as all this sounds—okay, as unrealistic as all of this *is*—the *Alien* movies portend a very real dynamic that takes place all around us every day. Within most of us is the embryo of an invader that has the potential to destroy us, along with those closest to us. It enters undetected. Its growth is unobserved. Then one day we hear ourselves saying something that we believe is totally uncharacteristic. Something that brings an expression of shock, maybe even hurt, to the face of someone we love. We put our hands over our mouths and exclaim, "I don't know where that came from!"

But to even the casual observer, it is obvious. *It came from within.* And chances are, it is likely to come again.

PART 1

CREATURE FEATURES

The heart is deceitful above all things,
    and desperately sick;
    who can understand it?

JEREMIAH 17:9, ESV

Miles: I take a dim view of watching my own
    destruction.

INVASION OF THE BODY SNATCHERS (1956)

Chapter One

IT CAME FROM WITHIN!

Dr. Jekyll: *Gentlemen like me have to be very careful of what we do or say.*

Dr. Jekyll and Mr. Hyde (1931)

Newt: *We'd better get back, 'cause it'll be dark soon, and they mostly come at night...mostly.*

Aliens (1986)

It came from within. But at first I wasn't sure where it came from. It was a Tuesday night. I was lying in bed, trying to go to sleep, when I felt a thump in my chest that actually shook my whole body. I sat up and looked over at Sandra to see if perhaps she had felt it too. No pain. No pressure. Just a larger-than-normal thump in my chest. I laid back down and tried to pretend it hadn't happened. And then it happened again.

This time I said, "Did you feel that?"

No answer.

As I laid there staring at the clock, I put my hand over my heart and tried to listen as well as feel my pulse. About a half minute later I noticed that my heart skipped a beat and then, THUMP! This happened over and over. About a minute of normal heartbeat and then nothing. And then the big *thump* that literally coursed through my entire body.

Needless to say, I didn't sleep much that night.

The next day I called my doctor. He sent me to the hospital with a prescription for this nifty device that records what's happening to your heart while you go about your normal routine. I say *normal*. There are a few "normal" activities I would advise anyone against trying while wearing such a device.

The following day I went back to the hospital and they plugged the device into a computer to see what they could find. An hour later the technician came out and informed me that I had an irregular heartbeat. I was shocked. "Really? An irregular heartbeat? You don't say. You mean my heart isn't supposed to miss a beat every minute and then make up for it with increased seismic intensity?"

Of course, I didn't *say* that. He was about to draw some blood, and I've always tried to stay on the good side of anyone who's about to poke me with a needle.

They ran some tests. A lot of tests. After a couple hours of blood work, an EKG, an ultrasound—I told them there was no way I was pregnant, but they insisted—and a chest X-ray, a doctor came in to see me. He sat down with his clipboard and started asking me all the usual questions. Eventually he came to the "What medications are you taking?" question. Ordinarily that's an easy one: "Nothing." But it just so happened that I was taking something for my annual case of poison ivy. I'm never certain how I got it, but I always manage to come down with it every spring. Truth is, I don't even know what poison ivy looks like—which may be part of my problem.

I tried to pronounce the name of the drug I was taking. After three or four failed attempts, the doctor deciphered what had been prescribed and wrote it down. Then he asked, "They didn't prescribe a steroid as well?" No, they hadn't. The reason being, I had insisted that my family doctor give me the steroid in the form of a shot. Two shots, actually. When I shared this bit of seemingly insignificant news with the doctor, he put down his pen and smiled. "I think I know what your problem is."

This was good news. Sandra has been wondering since we were married.

"What?" I asked.

"It's the steroids. You are going to be fine. Once it works its way through your system your heart will settle back down."

And you know what—he was right. The problem took care of itself.

THE THING WITH TWO HEARTS

As you have probably guessed from this story, I am not a doctor. And this is not a book about your physical heart. It's about your other heart.

You know, that invisible part of you that philosophers, poets, and preachers refer to all the time. That thing that got broken in the ninth grade when what's-her-name said she just wanted to be friends. I'm talking about that part of you that swells up with pride when you see your kids do something great. It's that thing that gets all nostalgic when you hear an old Journey tune (or whatever music served as the soundtrack for your senior year). It's that part of me that fills up when Sandra sits down next to me on the front row at church every Sunday morning. Amazing how that still happens after all these years...

And to be fair, the heart I'm talking about is also that part of me that wanted to wring the coach's neck for keeping my son on the bench throughout an entire all-star game.

The heart I'm speaking of is that mysterious, wonderful, confusing part of you that enables you to love, laugh, fear, and experience life. It is the sphere in which relationship happens. And it is the sphere in which relationships are broken.

DAMAGE CONTROL

Life can be hard on the heart. The world is full of outside influences that have the power to disrupt the rhythm of your heart. Most are subtle. Some may even appear to be necessary as protection from further disruptions. Over time you develop habits that slowly erode your heart's sensitivity. The inevitable pain and disappointment of life have

Have the inevitable pain and disappointment of life caused you to build walls around your heart?

caused you to set up walls around your heart. Much of this is understandable. But at the end of the day, there's no way around the truth: Your heart is out of sync with the rhythm it was created to maintain.

These disrupters that throw your heart out of sync are not like the steroid that eventually worked its way out of my system without any effort on my part. Those things that disrupt the rhythms of the invisible heart linger. If left alone, some will linger for a lifetime. After a while we come to accept these disrupters as part of us, part of our personality. And so we catch ourselves saying, "That's just the way I am." But you weren't always that way. And those closest to you know it.

So let me ask you, how are things with your heart?

Close the book and think for a moment. How are things with your heart? Not your career, your family, or your finances. Your heart. Chances are, you've never stopped to consider your heart. And why should you? There are meals to fix, calls to return, interviews to prepare for, and bills to pay. If at the end of the day you're all caught up with these things and someone asks, "How are things?" you can smile and sigh and say, "Fine."

But this is a different question.

It is a more important question.

And yes, it is an *awkward* question.

ANOTHER ME

Perhaps the major reason we rarely stop to monitor our hearts is that it was never encouraged. As children, we were taught instead to monitor our behavior. In other words, we were taught to *behave*. If we behaved properly, good things happened, regardless of what was going on in our hearts. If we misbehaved, not-so-good things happened. My parents believed in spanking. So the not-so-good things got my attention early. I modified my behavior so as to avoid pain, and I've been doing that ever since. I bet you have too.

Years ago a buddy and I decided to move a road sign. We thought it would be funny to route traffic up an entrance ramp that led to a highway that was under construction and not opened yet. As a result, I spent the good portion of a night in jail. So I modified my behavior. I never moved another road sign.

Pain, embarrassment, fines, and spankings are generally considered effective ways to focus an individual's attention on his or her behavior. Consequently, you and I have become much better at monitoring our behavior than our hearts.

But it is not just the avoidance of pain that drives us. Good behavior can be rewarding. As a professional Christian—a pastor, by trade—I am paid to be good. So I have learned to modify my words and behavior so as not to damage my reputation and, thus, my career.

We have become much better at monitoring our behavior than our hearts.

You've no doubt done the same thing. Whatever your job, there are some things you just won't do. Not because you don't want to, but because of the professional ramifications. Perhaps there are some words and phrases you won't use, in spite of the fact that they would accurately convey what you are feeling. I'll bet there are some people you pretend to like because it is beneficial to you. And all of that is fine. More than fine, it's necessary. After all, like my buddy Charlie is fond of saying, everybody's got to eat and live indoors.

But all this pretending can be problematic because pretending allows you to ignore the true condition of your heart. As long as you say the right thing and do the right thing, you're tempted to believe that all is well. That's what your childhood experience taught you. But when your public performance becomes too far removed from who you are in your heart, you've been set up for trouble. Eventually your heart—the *real* you—will outpace your attempts to monitor and modify everything you say and do. The unresolved issues stirring around undetected in your heart will eventually work their way to the surface. Specifically, they will seep into your actions, your character, and your relationships. If your heart continues to go unmonitored, whatever "thing" is growing in there will worsen to the point that you are no longer able to contain it with carefully managed words and behaviors.

So let me ask you again: How's your heart?

SLIPPAGE

Maybe you've already noticed things starting to slip a bit. Maybe you've always been able to contain your anger, but lately there's a edge in your voice that scares even you. And what about those occasional outbursts that slip through your normally ironclad façade?

You know you ought to be happy for Frank on his promotion, but for some reason you're not. The truth is, Frank represents that person from your past who bought something or won something or was given something you wanted, and now you find yourself resenting Frank for it.

Ladies, how about your sister-in-law who wears those jeans you know better than to try and fit into. She looks great, but you aren't about to let her know that. But why? Why does it bother you? You know it shouldn't. So you behave like everything is okay. But it's not.

These are merely symptoms of a deeper struggle. Your heart is under assault, and it could be that you are losing. Primarily through neglect. After all, nobody ever told us to keep a close check on our hearts.

Evidence of an internal battle are statements like:

"I can't believe I just said that."

"I don't know where that came from."

"I can't believe I did that."

"That's not like me."

HEART EXAM

Cardiologists use a procedure called an arteriogram to diagnose the health of a patient's heart. An arteriogram is an X-ray of the arteries taken after a dye is injected into the bloodstream. The dye allows doctors to pinpoint blockage in the arteries that serve as conduits carrying blood from the heart.

If blockage is discovered, a skilled cardiologist is able to insert a stent through an artery in the patient's leg, navigate it up into the heart, and open up the blood vessels so that blood can again flow freely to blocked or damaged regions. It is an amazing procedure to watch on video. You can actually see the dye making its way through the arteries and then stopping when it reaches an area that is blocked. Even an untrained eye can spot the problem area once the dye has been injected—it is that obvious.

But apart from an arteriogram, a life-threatening heart problem can go undetected for years. An individual who has blockage will experience symptoms, but these symptoms may not seem to be directly associated with the heart. Arterial blockage can manifest itself through back pain, inability to sleep, anxiety, loss of appetite, indigestion, nausea, vision change, even loss of memory.

What were we just talking about? Oh yes.

All of these are symptoms that can be and often are treated as isolated issues unrelated to the health of the heart. And the right medication can take the edge off most of these symptoms. The problem, of course, is that treating the symptoms masks the real culprit. Worse, it delays treatment of the problem, thus leaving the problem to worsen.

HEART OF THE MATTER

Likewise, we are tempted to treat the ancillary, symptomatic challenges that stem from an unhealthy heart while ignoring the deeper issues. But as is the case with the physical heart, eventually the root problem will become a real problem. And just as a heart attack has the potential to destroy your body, so spiritual heart disease has the potential to destroy you and squeeze the life out of your most valuable relationships.

So for the next couple hundred pages, we are going to do some poking around. I'm going to do my best to expose your heart to the penetrating light of God's truth. Like the dye used in an arteriogram, truth can help us to pinpoint the blockage in our spiritual condition. Once the problem area has been identified, the solutions are usually pretty obvious. Actually, the solutions are quite simple. But first we must familiarize ourselves with the most common blockages, their causes, and their symptoms.

These enemies of the heart can destroy your relationships, your character, and even your faith.

In these pages I will deal with four primary enemies of the heart—four life-blocking agents that can become lodged there for various reasons. Each has the potential to erode your relationships, your character, and even your faith. We will spend several chapters looking at each of these in detail. I will then challenge you to embrace four new habits. I often refer to these as "habits of the heart"—habits that exercise the heart and allow it to maintain the rhythm for which it was designed. Each of these habits specifically addresses one of four maladies that can infect your heart. Three of the four habits will probably sound familiar; the fourth one may be new to you. When applied consistently, these four disciplines will bring healing and wholeness to your heart, whatever your current condition. There is some evidence to suggest that these habits can positively impact your physical health as well. Personally, I believe these habits have the potential to change everything.

If this all sounds too good to be true, let me remind you of a declaration God made generations ago that is still true and extraordinarily relevant today. He claimed that he could give a man or woman a new heart (see Ezekiel 36:26). The interesting thing is that he said this to a people who already had God's List of Top Ten Behaviors to guide them. But clearly it wasn't enough for them to know *what* to do; they needed to change from the inside out in order to follow through. Each of them needed, as we need, to drop the public persona and become one whole and healthy person.

What we need is a heart that can keep pace with our outward obedience.

TAKE TWO

If you grew up going to the kind of church I grew up in, the notion of God's still needing to do some work in your heart may cause a bit of inner tension. Perhaps you prayed a prayer some time ago inviting Jesus to come into your heart. And like me, you may have assumed that once he was in, all was well. I mean, Jesus has made himself at home in my heart, so everything is copasetic, right? But somewhere along the way each of us is forced to face the painful truth that all is not well. So we pray the prayer a second or third time for fear that the first one didn't take. And yet we continue to see disturbing signs that our heart isn't entirely new. So what's up?

What's up is this: What God begins at the moment of our salvation is not completed in that same moment. I bet you already knew that about yourself, didn't you? If you didn't know it, I'd bet your best friend does. At the risk of oversimplifying, let me put it this way: Jesus may have moved into your heart, but he may not have been given full access. That's why as happy as you are about being forgiven, you're not always willing to extend forgiveness to others. That's a heart thing. As excited as you are about the success you're experiencing, you aren't always excited about the success someone else is enjoying. That's a heart thing too. Both are evidence that God has not completed in you what he has begun. You're still a work in progress. There is still some heart work to be done.

One last thing before we move on. Your heart did not arrive at its present condition overnight. It will not become healthy overnight either. You can't overcome in an instant the effects of years of blockage caused by guilt, anger, greed, and jealousy. Adopting new habits of the heart is a process, but it is a process that will yield some immediate results. My hope is that these immediate dividends will encourage and motivate you to continue cultivating these new habits until you arrive at a place where your Creator desires and made you to be.

Chapter Two

ALL IS NOT
AS IT SEEMS

Dr. Morbius: *My evil self is at the door, and I have no power
to stop it!*

Forbidden Planet (1956)

The Vicar: *Beware! Beware the beast within!*

Wallace & Gromit: The Curse of the Were-Rabbit (2005)

If you are an NBA fan you will no doubt recognize the name Peter
Maravich. If you are like me, a sports moron, perhaps you won't.
If not, don't worry. This will be quick and painless.

Long before there was a Doctor J or a Magic or an Air Jordan,
there was a Pistol. Pistol Pete Maravich. He was a skinny white guard
from LSU who treated the basketball court like a stage. When Pete
rocketed onto the court, the fans went nuts. His presence turned the
game into a show. He was the master of the behind-the-back, over-
the-shoulder, "look away" pass. "If I have a choice whether to do the

show or throw a straight pass," said Maravich, a three-time All-American, "and we're going to get the basket either way, I'm going to do the show."

While Pistol Pete is the NCAA Division I all-time leading scorer, it was his gamesmanship that dazzled and bewildered the fans that flocked to watch his creative genius. With the ball seemingly connected to his fingers by an invisible string, Pistol Pete's skillful dribbling often left defenders looking foolish, the ball smoothly moving between his legs, behind his back, and through the smallest of defensive openings.

At a summer camp, legendary coach Lefty Driesell assured him that the great Oscar Robertson succeeded without flamboyant passes. Maravich responded that he wanted to be a millionaire, "and they don't pay you a million dollars for two-hand chest passes." At LSU, where Pistol Pete played for his father, Press, he set still-standing Division I records with his 44.5 points per game for a season (1969–70), a 44.2 scoring average for his career (1967–70), and 3,667 total points. During his NBA career, Maravich was selected to five all-star teams and was later voted among the league's fifty greatest players in history.

"Pistol" wore his hair long and shaggy and his socks seemingly two sizes too large, but he produced huge numbers. Rail-thin and in fantastic physical shape, Maravich looked as if he could play for days, never tiring as he wowed fans and players alike with his "street ball" style.

But on January 5, 1988, only a few years removed from playing grueling 70-plus game schedules, while playing a pickup basketball game with a group that included Focus on the Family head James Dobson—Maravich was scheduled to appear on Dobson's radio show later that day—Pistol Pete collapsed and died of a heart attack at the age of 40. An autopsy revealed that his death was due to a previously undiagnosed congenital heart defect—he had been born with only one coronary artery instead of the normal two.

Stories like those of Pistol Pete or Reggie White—pictures of seemingly perfect athleticism who tragically and suddenly dropped dead of a heart attack at a relatively young age—cause us to come to grips with a sobering truth: A person's physical prowess doesn't always reflect the health of his or her heart. To assume too much about a person's cardiovascular health from simply observing that individual's physical abilities can be fatal.

Conversely, you probably know someone whose idea of a well-balanced meal is a box of Krispy Kreme donuts chased with a six-pack of Diet Coke. His heart, however, is miraculously in mint condition. Like a fine "Swill" watch, it just keeps right on ticking no matter how much it is abused or neglected. Again, behavior is not always an accurate indicator of what's going on inside.

THE WARNING SIGNS

As we noted earlier, when you have a heart problem, you don't necessarily know you have a heart problem. Sometimes there are no noticeable symptoms. When there are symptoms, they may appear to be unrelated to the cardiovascular system. Some are fortunate enough to discover they have a heart problem during the process of trying to find relief for these symptoms, but heart patients rarely begin their medical journey with a cardiologist. Generally speaking, people don't track down a cardiologist until their family doctor recommends they do so.

Now, our bodies are uniquely made to give us distress signals when things are not right. Like flares against a clear night sky, these signals warn of impending danger. Signals that should not be ignored. But these signals need diagnosing. And they can easily be misread and misinterpreted.

When you open the Scriptures, both in the Old and the New Testaments you find a similar concept related to the health of your other heart—your other heart being that intangible part of you that loves, hates, palpitates, and melts at the sight of certain people. The Bible attributes a great many evils to this other heart. Things we would normally not associate with our hearts at all. Like the man who habitually reaches for the Mylanta when his cardio-induced "indigestion" wakes him up, we tend to reach for remedies to address our symptoms without ever really dealing with the root problem. And so the symptoms never seem to go away.

"Pear-haps" an illustration will help.

ROOT PROBLEMS

Imagine for a moment that you've purchased a home with a large pear tree in the yard that yields an abundance of pears each year. So abundant, in fact, that the pear tree cannot bear the weight of all of the fruit and your yard becomes a sea of pears. Normally, that wouldn't be a problem, except for the fact that every time you walk through your backyard you come into the house with mashed pear stuck to the bottom of your shoes. Worse, when you cut your grass, the fallen pears are transformed into supersonic projectiles—fruity missiles that target your car, your house, and your neighbor's fence. If that wasn't bad enough, rotting pears in the summer sun smell awful, attract bugs, and kill the grass.

So what do you do? You could always grab a bucket and pick up all the pears. That would solve your problem for a couple of weeks, perhaps for a season. But come next spring, you will be right back where you started. Chances are, if you wanted to rid yourself of the pear problem for good you wouldn't opt for simply gathering up the fallen pears. You would take a more permanent approach.

Yet, as we are about to see, the first approach is precisely the way we tend to tackle our heart problems. We keep picking up and apologizing for our insensitive words and our inappropriate behaviors. We swear to ourselves, and maybe to the people around us, that we will never act that way again. And we mean it. Then we repeat our mis-

take. And we pull out our basket and pick 'em all up and dole out another round of apologies.

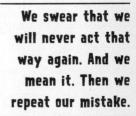

We swear that we will never act that way again. And we mean it. Then we repeat our mistake.

If we are well read we might even have a good explanation as to why it's so hard for us to break the cycle. "After all, our parents...blah blah blah...and the pressures at work...blah blah blah..." And on and on we go, blaming and explaining. But in the end, nothing really changes.

If you don't like the fruit that keeps cluttering up your backyard, the only real solution is to dig up the tree by the roots and eliminate the issue once and for all. If you deal with the source, you have dealt with the problem.

Aren't you glad I cleared that up for you?

Okay, while I'm insulting your intelligence with the obvious, let me go one step further. We aren't surprised when pear trees continue to drop pears. You wouldn't be surprised to find apples strewn all over an apple grove. You expect to step on a few pecans if you walk under a pecan tree. In each case you know the source and you know what has to be done to rid the ground of needless fruit.

So tell me this: What is the source of all the inappropriate behaviors and hurtful words that litter the ground around you? Specifically, the ones that dropped out of your mouth and were produced by your hands. You know what I'm talking about. All that stuff you keep trying to sweep up and explain away that keeps coming back. What is the source?

While you're pondering that, ponder this as well: What is the solution? If the source were simply a few behavioral habits, you would have conquered them already. If the solution were "try harder," you would have licked the problem by now. So what's the source and what's the solution?

Unlike an overbearing fruit tree, we can't exactly cut ourselves down and have ourselves hauled away. But let's face it, there may be people who have packed up and moved away from *you* because they were tired of being assaulted with your bad fruit. And chances are, you have done some moving yourself when you realized that someone close to you wasn't ever going to change.

So what's the source and what's the solution?

Let's ask the question a different way.

OOPS!

Has this ever happened to you? You say something that is entirely out of character for you and you cover your mouth as if to say, "I can't believe I said that." Perhaps you even say, "Where did *that* come from?" People look at you like, "Yikes! Where *did* that come from?"

So where *did* that come from? Don't know?

Want to take a wild guess?

You think that outburst was an exception. And in one way it was. It was an exception to your general rule of not allowing what's in your heart to be exposed to the rest of the world. But as we will discover in the next chapter, that embarrassing outburst was not an *exception* to what is in your heart. Indeed, it was a *reflection* of what's really swirling around down there.

We have all grown very adept at covering for our hearts. In fact, we are so good at it that most of us have no idea just how corrupt we really are. But every once in a while our heart goes public. We swear we didn't mean it. But the truth is, we just didn't mean to *say* it.

TRUTH BE TOLD

Remember the Jim Carrey character in the movie *Liar Liar*? If you didn't see it—and I'm not necessarily recommending that you do— Carrey played the part of Fletcher, a lawyer and pathological liar whose son wishes that his father would tell the truth for one whole day. Magically,

> **What if it suddenly became impossible for you to cover up all the junk you normally hide from the rest of humanity?**

for twenty-four hours it becomes impossible for Fletcher to lie about anything. Suddenly his heart is exposed—as in, *completely* exposed. His mouth becomes an unfiltered mirror of what's been stirring around in his heart all along. Fletcher's biggest asset (his mouth) becomes his biggest liability. He can't cover up anything. He's exposed.

If it suddenly became impossible for us to cover up all the junk we normally hide from the rest of humanity, I have a feeling we would all get real motivated to deal with the source of what ails us. If the filters came off, we would no doubt be relentless about repairing the condition of our hearts. Like the man who discovers that he is a couple of cheeseburgers away from a major heart attack, we would reprioritize everything in order to address this pressing issue.

DON'T DO AS I DO

But it's not just our words that surprise us, is it? How many times have you caught yourself doing something you know you shouldn't do? Something you are fundamentally against. Something you would readily condemn if somebody else did it. In my case, things I've preached against! And then we mumble to ourselves, "I don't know why I did that? That's not like me."

So where *did that* come from? What's the source?

Did the devil make you do it?

Now there's an idea. Maybe it was the devil! Maybe we are not really responsible, or at least not completely responsible, for our actions. Maybe there *is* someone else to blame after all.

Interestingly, the Bible does not encourage us to try and trace our uncharacteristic behavior back to Satan. No, it points us in another direction entirely.

I can't blame you—or myself, for that matter—for trying to deflect the blame. Nobody wants to admit to having heart problems. It sounds so serious. I know I feel better if I think my occasional slip-ups are purely behavioral. After all, nobody's perfect. But if you tell me my heart is faulty or in need of repair…well, that hurts. Now I feel like a *bad* person, like I'm a candidate for some sort of rehabilitation program.

I worked with high school students for fifteen years, and I can't remember all the times I counseled parents whose kids had gotten into some kind of trouble. Inevitably, Mom and Dad would say something like, "He's a good kid. He's got a good heart. He just got into a little trouble."

Wrong.

Yes, he's a cute kid. He's a talented kid. But he's not a "good" kid. Good kids do good things, kind of like pear trees produce pears. The reality was, their child's heart was fouled up. Every one of these kids had a heart problem, not just a behavior problem. And the parents who recognized the root problem and responded accordingly were always rewarded with improvement in their child's behavior. But the parents who wouldn't allow themselves to face the painful truth found themselves dealing with the same kinds of issues over and over. Putting a kid on restriction does nothing for his or her heart; it only delays further misadventures.

FRIENDLY FIRE

Let's get back to you. Here's something the people around you know that you may not have clued into yet: The people closest to you routinely catch the flak thrown off by the explosive stuff you normally work so hard to keep hidden. It may not come out on the golf course. It doesn't come out among casual acquaintances. And it almost never comes out in a social setting. What's in your heart comes out at home, where you've turned off the "safety" and let down your defenses. That's when the heart exposes itself in the most negative ways to the people you love the most.

We hurt most who we love the most.

Bad grammar, painful truth.

But there is a solution. We need to change. We need to change from the inside out. It won't do us any good to guard our behavior more closely. Our words and deeds are simply a gauge of what's going on inside. They indicate where we are, where we aren't, and where we are headed. But the real culprit is the heart. That's where the real transformation must take place.

Not convinced? Read on…

Chapter Three

WHEN RULES COLLIDE

Dr. Emanuel: *The fools! Here we are so close to solving the mystery of life and death, and they worry about their precious laws.*

<small>CURSE OF THE FACELESS MAN (1958)</small>

Dr. Frankenstein: *Speak! I know you have a civil tongue in your head because I sewed it back myself.*

<small>I WAS A TEENAGE FRANKENSTEIN (1957)</small>

Growing up I wasn't allowed to say "darn." "Darn" sounded too much like "damn." At least, that was the reason I was given. I couldn't say "gosh" or "gee" for pretty much the same reason. "Gosh" sounded like "God," and "gee" sounded like "Jesus."

Now to a kid these aren't very compelling reasons not to use those words. It seemed to me I should get credit for *not* saying "damn" or "God." Regardless, those were the rules. And the punishment? Well that didn't make much sense either. My folks told me that an infraction would result in my mouth being washed out with soap.

I couldn't picture it. But it didn't sound like something I wanted to experience. So I promised not to say anything that sounded like anything I wasn't supposed to say. And for a long time I didn't. Alas, all good things must come to an end.

One afternoon I was in the front yard playing with my buddies from the neighborhood. Buddies who, by the way, never said "darn" either, but for different reasons. Anyway, we were engaged in the heat of bicycle wars when I lost myself and shouted, "Get that darn bike out of my way!"

Now, I don't know how it is that from inside the house my mother was able to distinguish my voice from all the other young male voices in the yard. But she did. The next thing I knew, she was standing at the door. Very calmly she said, "Andy, please come in the house."

Unbeknownst to me, my mother was as unprepared as I was for what happened next. Washing my mouth out with soap was actually my dad's idea, and he wasn't home. He wasn't even in town! So Mom had the objectionable task of washing my mouth out with soap—something she had never done and had no idea how to do.

And all this over a word that wasn't even a bad word. It just *sounded* like one.

She marched me into the bathroom, took my toothbrush out of the medicine cabinet, raked it several times across a bar of soap, and proceeded to brush my teeth. I just about threw up. Mom didn't look too well herself.

To this day I don't know if this particular punishment was designed to be carried out in that way, but I do know this: The toothbrush method is effective. And that was the only time I ever had my mouth washed out with soap. "Darn" has been absent from my vocabulary ever since.

RULES FOR KEEPING RULES

My parents were not the first to establish a secondary rule to keep someone from breaking a primary rule. Thousands of years ago certain religious leaders were making a career out of it. By the time Jesus arrived on the scene, more than five hundred rules had been added to the laws handed down to Moses by God himself. This ever-growing body of regulations was called "the Tradition of the Elders." Its sole purpose was to prevent the Jewish populace from accidentally breaking one of the original commandments. For example, the Law of Moses forbade commerce on the Sabbath; so they added a clause that forbade the handling of money on the Sabbath, thereby ensuring that no one would violate the original Sabbath law. Over time, the religious leaders had assigned to these traditions a status equal to the Law of Moses.

To the continual chagrin of the Pharisees and Sadducees, Jesus paid very little attention to their traditions. While he and his disciples observed the Mosaic Code, Jesus seemed to go out of his way to violate the man-made laws of the Jewish hierarchy. The religious authorities would often point to these infractions as evidence of his blatant disregard for the Law, thereby refuting his claim to be a spokesman for God.

Matthew records one such incident. Interestingly, the rule that got Jesus into hot water on this occasion was a rule we have around *our* house. He forgot—well, I guess Jesus never *forgot* anything. He *decided* not to wash his hands before he ate. And his disciples followed suit.

This was troublesome to the Pharisees, just like it is to my wife.

According to the Tradition of the Elders, everybody was supposed to wash from the tips of their fingers all the way down to the elbows before partaking of food. Persnickety as it may seem, the Tradition of the Elders went to great lengths to explain how one should wash his hands before eating. Beyond basic hygiene, this rule was designed to keep people from accidentally becoming ceremonially unclean—that is, it kept a person from unintentionally putting the wrong thing, or something that had *touched* a wrong thing, into his or her body.

One night Jesus didn't wash his hands before he ate. This was troublesome to the Pharisees, just like it is to my wife.

But washing your hands before a meal was not required by the Law of Moses. Sure, it's a good idea, but the rabbis had made it a standard for righteousness. Over time this rule had taken on the same significance in the Jewish community as the original laws handed down at Mount Sinai.

But Jesus ignored this rule and didn't insist that his followers apply it either. Here's how the whole thing went down, as recorded in Matthew 15:1–20.

> Then some Pharisees and teachers of the law came to Jesus from Jerusalem and asked, "Why do your disciples break the tradition of the elders? They don't wash their hands before they eat!"

Clearly, these guys needed something to do. Here they are, standing in the presence of a man who heals the sick and calms the seas with his words, and they're in a tizzy over the fact that he doesn't wash his hands before meals.

Jesus answers their question with a question: "And why do you break the command of God for the sake of your tradition?"

He turns it right back around on them. The Pharisees accuse him of ignoring the rules they had tacked onto the Law. Jesus in turn accuses them of breaking God's law in order to keep one of their tacked-on rules. Then before they can respond, he launches into a scathing minisermon. He doesn't hold back. Calls 'em hypocrites. He accuses them of nullifying the word of God for the sake of their homemade traditions. It was brutal.

As soon as he finishes with the Pharisees, Jesus turns his attention to the disciples (who were probably busy high-fiving each other over the spectacle of seeing the religious referees beaten at their own game). He picks up on the cleanliness theme the Pharisees have introduced:

"Don't you see that whatever enters the mouth goes into the stomach and then out of the body?"

Now there's an insight. What enters a person's mouth will ultimately pass through the body… I doubt anybody wrote that down, except Matthew. But now that he has their undivided attention, Jesus drives home his point.

"But the things that come out of the mouth come from the heart, and these make a man 'unclean.'"

His point? God is not nearly as concerned about what goes *in* our mouths as he is about what comes *out* of our mouths. God is not nearly as concerned about what goes *into* our bodies as what comes *out* of our bodies. This was new territory for the Jews; they were extremely cautious about what they put in their mouths. Now Jesus was saying that God was more offended by what came out than what went in.

But it was this comment that must have gotten their attention: "the things that come out of the mouth come from the heart."

The heart? Everything that comes out of the mouth comes from the *heart? Everything?* Did he really mean that? At first glance, I'm inclined to disagree. Surely, not everything that comes out of my mouth originates in my heart?

If you're like me, there have been plenty of times when you said stuff you didn't really mean. Again, we've all covered our mouths and muttered, "I don't know where *that* came from!" But apparently, Jesus would respond, "I do. It came from within. It came from your heart."

But it gets worse.

Jesus goes on to say that the heart is not only responsible for our words but for our deeds as well:

"For out of the heart come evil thoughts, murder, adultery, sexual immorality, theft, false testimony, slander. These are what make a man 'unclean'; but eating with unwashed hands does not make him 'unclean.'"

Evil thoughts? I thought these originated in my…mind. If Jesus is right—and I'm betting he is—my mind is not the source of all my thoughts. It goes deeper than that. My evil thoughts originate in my heart. Take a look at the other items on his list. They are all actions, deeds, and behaviors. And they all come from the heart.

MONITOR THIS

The implications of this are huge. As we touched on in the introduction, our tendency is to monitor our behavior while pretty much ignoring our hearts. After all, how do you monitor your heart? Keeping an eye on my behavior is easy. Besides, I have lots of help with that. I can't get too far off base in my behavior without somebody drawing it to my attention. But my heart? That seems a bit more complicated.

But if the items on Jesus' list emanate from the heart, then clearly we need a new monitoring strategy. After all, if we knew how to monitor our hearts, if we knew how to deal with trouble at its source, then perhaps we would see a marked improvement in our behavior. Makes you wonder why no one ever taught us to do this.

ALL OF A SUDDEN

Jesus wasn't the first to point out the importance of the heart. Nearly a thousand years earlier, Solomon echoed Jesus' concern when he wrote, "Watch over your heart with all diligence, for from it flow the springs of life" (Proverbs 4:23, NASB). Here we are actually commanded to "watch over" or guard our hearts. Why? Because our lives—i.e., words and behaviors—flow from our hearts. The heart is the source.

Somehow what's in our hearts, good or bad, is eventually translated into words and deeds. That's a bit scary. Especially since it's so hard to know what's going on in there. For example, when we hear or see something and suddenly we are overwhelmed with emotion, we think, *That really touched my heart*. But we are always surprised when it happens, aren't we? Why? Perhaps because we're so out of touch with our hearts. On the flip side, we've all seen and heard things that should have affected us emotionally, and...nothing. No response. And we wonder, *What's wrong with me? Why was everyone else impacted and I just stood there, unmoved?* Perhaps you've even been accused of being "hard-hearted" or having "a heart of stone." If you are a guy, you may have even taken pride in the fact that your heart is not easily moved. But is that a good thing? And is that even true?

> **What's in our hearts, good or bad, will eventually come out as words and deeds.**

The heart is such a mystery. In fact, one prophet asked of the heart, "Who can understand it?" (Jeremiah 17:9). Good question. The implication is, nobody. With which I readily concur. And even if we do begin to understand it, we certainly can't control it—which is all the more reason we need to learn to monitor it. Like the seismic activity of a dormant volcano, what you don't know *can* hurt you. If you have suffered the consequences from anything on Jesus' from-the-heart list, you know that to be a fact.

Suddenly someone files for divorce.

Suddenly a kid's grades drop and his attitude changes.

Suddenly a harmless pastime becomes a destructive habit.

Out of nowhere devastating words pierce the soul of an unsuspecting loved one.

We've all seen it, felt it, even caused it. Just as Jesus predicted, what originates in the secret place won't always remain a secret. Eventually it finds its way into our homes, offices, and neighborhoods.

Okay, so we are all volcanoes waiting to erupt. Now what? How do we combat something we can't even see? How do we guard—or maybe it would be more appropriate to say, *guard against*—our hearts? How do we monitor what's going on in that secret place that has the potential to go public at any moment?

I'm glad you asked. That's what we are going to spend the next few hours discovering together.

Chapter Four

THE DAY MY WORLD STOOD STILL

Ro-Man: *Yes! To be like the hu-man! To laugh! Feel! Want!*
  Why are these things not in the plan?

ROBOT MONSTER (1953)

Wake me up inside.
Wake me up inside.
Call my name and save me from the dark.

EVANESCENCE, "BRING ME TO LIFE"

North of Atlanta there is an intersection where two major highways come together: I-285 and I-85. When I say intersection, I'm not talking about a traffic light with a turn lane. This monstrosity of twentieth-century engineering spans several miles and includes innumerable overpasses and exit ramps. I've driven over, under, and through this interchange hundreds of times and I still have to pay careful attention to the signs lest I find myself headed right back in the direction from which I came.

Years ago when the interchange opened, a local radio station held a contest to nickname this massive tangle of concrete and steel. My favorite entry was "The Car-Strangled Spanner." The name that stuck, however, was "Spaghetti Junction." When you look at it from the sky, the name is certainly fitting. And as confusing as it is to navigate, it is actually an extraordinarily efficient traffic hub—unless you happen to be passing through between 4:00 PM and 6:00 PM. During this time of day, Spaghetti Junction becomes a multilane parking lot. Everything comes to a standstill. All hopes of being home for dinner, early for a ball game, or on time for a meeting are dashed.

Just about everybody in the Atlanta metropolitan area has, at one time or another, driven into Spaghetti Junction with a smile on their face and a song in their heart only to find themselves driving out an hour later with visions of selling everything they own and moving to the country. The good news is, everybody eventually makes it out. The bad new is, few people come out with the same attitude they went in with. In my case, the longer I sit there, the more my attitude deteriorates.

THE OTHER HUB

The heart is a hub as well. Everything we experience is processed through our hearts, the good and the bad. Life comes at us from all directions, but it all gets channeled through our hearts. Unfortunately, our negative experiences have a tendency to get stuck there. Eventually they make their way out through our words and deeds; but because of the delay between entry and exit, we often have a difficult time making the connection.

So we are mad but don't know why. We are discontent but can find no real reason to feel that way. We're resentful toward certain types of people, though they have done nothing to deserve it. We are jealous while knowing all the time that it is foolish to dislike somebody for having something we don't. None of these things make any sense, but they are real. And left unchecked they have the potential to drive us into self-destructive and relationship-wrecking behavior patterns.

So maybe Jesus was right. Maybe all that junk we don't like about ourselves really does come "from the heart."

CLOGGED ARTERIES

Maybe Jesus was right? Of course he was right.

The heart seeps into *every* conversation. It dictates every relationship. Our very lives emanate from the heart. We live, parent, lead, relate, romance, confront, react, respond, instruct, manage, problem solve, and love from the heart. Our hearts impact the intensity of our communication. Our hearts have the potential to exaggerate our sensitivities and insensitivities. Every arena of life intersects with what's going on in our hearts. Everything passes through on its way to wherever it is going. Everything.

Thus the need to monitor our hearts. Even if life were a level playing field, clearly we would need to keep an eye on what's going on in that invisible but vital part of our being. But life is not a level playing field.

Let's face it, life is not always kind. Everyone experiences a measure of hurt and rejection, some more than others. As a result of these unavoidable realities, unpleasant things become lodged in

our hearts. We have even developed language to describe this phe-
nomenon:

"I'll never trust another man."
"I'll never love again."
"I'll never give my heart to anyone."
"I don't need anybody."
"I'm not letting anybody in."
"She broke my heart."
"He wounded me."

Or when talking about people whose hearts have been damaged, we
may say:

"He's hard-hearted."
"You'll never get to know her. She has walls."
"He has trust issues."
"She's cold."
"Hugging him is like hugging an ice cube."

The earliest of our wounds are often inflicted during childhood.
At the time, our age prevents us from accurately processing exactly
what we feel; all we know is that it's bad and we don't ever want to
feel that way again. Ever. If the hurt is repeated, we begin to develop
coping mechanisms. We have to. The natural response to pain is to
stop it and, once we've stopped it, to prevent it from ever happening
again. This is true of physical as well as emotional pain. And in some
cases we will go to extremes to stop our pain. Extreme pain calls for
extreme measures.

PAIN WITHOUT A NAME

I was present when my oldest son got his feelings hurt for the first time. It was terrible. Andrew was almost four. We were having a party, and an adult was kidding around with him about something. Suddenly, Andrew just closed up. I had never seen that expression on his face before, but I knew exactly what had happened. He turned around without a word and walked into the living room. I followed him, and when he saw me Andrew just stared at me with a look of pain and confusion. He was feeling something he had never felt before, and he had no idea of what to do with those feelings. I sat down on the couch and extended my arms. He just stood there. I reached out and grabbed him and just held on. There was no point in trying to explain to him that the person who made the comment was just kidding. That was irrelevant. These were new feelings with no name and no place to go. So I just held on.

After a few minutes I stood him in front of me and said, "That hurt on the inside, didn't it." At that point Andrew burst out crying. And I was so glad he did. I'm no psychologist, but I know the danger of allowing something to get lodged in your heart. And I wanted to keep this little boy's heart free of debris as long as possible. His tears cleansed his little heart, and I just held him as they flowed.

> The natural response to pain, physical or emotional, is to stop it—and prevent it from ever happening again.

Unfortunately for most of us, nobody was there when we received our first wound. So we just carried it around with us, determined not to let it happen again. By adolescence we all had wounded hearts.

Between the little jabs from our friends, our parents, our teachers, our coaches, and our adversaries at school, there was no way to avoid it.

My Achilles' heel was my teeth. I had terrible buckteeth. My teeth were so bad that my orthodontist won an award for creating a gadget to fix my mouth. Not just my teeth—my entire mouth. He actually kept my before-and-after impressions on display in his office. Anybody who doubted his credentials needed only to check out my impressions to be duly impressed with his skill.

I took more than my fair share of abuse in the years before braces. I was so wounded, I refused to smile for pictures. In every picture from fourth grade to sixth grade, I'm either crying or frowning. Kids told me I looked funny, and I believed them. I still have a difficult time smiling in front of a camera.

You probably have a story or two yourself. They may even seem silly now. But they weren't silly then. Long after we slim down, grow into our feet, figure out what to do with our hair, and move beyond the years of acne, the memories and scars remain. I can still remember specific names kids called me in the sixth grade. In fact, that's about all I can remember about the sixth grade.

I feel pretty confident in saying that nobody gets through middle school without a wound or two.

SELF-INFLICTED WOUNDS

But others aren't always to blame. The junk that gets lodged in our hearts comes from a variety of sources. In fact, sometimes we are our own worst enemy.

For example, *secrets* can damage the heart. I have counseled dozens of people who had hidden habits or were harboring secrets from their past. These secrets had caused them to build walls in their relationships. In many cases, their personal secrets caused them to become unjustifiably suspicious of those closest to them. That's because we usually suspect in others what we are guilty of ourselves. In time their secrets took a toll. These men and women felt guilty, and they carried that guilt into all their relationships.

A similar dynamic occurs with shame. When shame becomes lodged in our hearts, it eventually impacts our words and behaviors. The extreme example is the adult who suddenly remembers from childhood a chapter of abuse, years after the incident occurred. Anyone who has been sexually abused or is married to an abuse victim knows the damage done to the heart.

> **None of us reach adulthood without a few dings to the heart.**

These are just a few examples. There are many more. We will touch on the more common ones later on. My point is that none of us reach adulthood without a few dings to the heart. Our response to those dings determines the condition of our hearts. We cannot control how people treat us. We cannot stop their hurtful words. But we can monitor their effects on our hearts. And perhaps, as we will see, we can reverse the damage and keep our hearts free from further destructive debris.

I, MONSTER

Okay, I realize the last couple of paragraphs got a little…clinical. Don't worry. I have no intention of reintroducing you to your inner child. You will have to pay somebody else big bucks for that.

But maybe you're starting to wonder, "Is this really all that important?" Well, no, it's not—that is, if you live on an island and don't plan
to interact with anyone. If that's the case, the condition of your heart
is largely irrelevant.

But if you're like me and you actually plan on trying to sustain
relationships with other people on planet earth, then yes, this is an
important subject. Why? Because heart issues always take their toll on
relationships. Specifically, heart issues impact an individual's ability to
initiate and maintain intimate relationships. By intimacy, I'm not referring only to sexual relationships, although I am including them.

Heart issues make intimacy difficult to maintain because intimacy revolves around knowing and being known. People with
shrapnel lodged in their hearts from something in their past don't
really want to be known. Being known is tantamount to being
"found out" or "discovered." That's a terrifying notion to somebody
with secrets. So they build walls. They respond defensively. You can
get close, but there is a limit. And if you push too hard, if you insist
on getting in—prepare yourself. For out of their mouth pours the
junk that always pours out of a mouth connected to a wounded
heart. And they will insist that *you* are the problem.

Carriers of the four parasites we are about to discuss have a difficult time looking in the mirror. They already did that, and they
didn't like what they saw. And every time you remind them—intentionally or unintentionally—you will reap the consequences. And in
time, their issues may very well become yours. The old adage is true:
Hurt people hurt people. And we could add, …*who hurt people, who
hurt people*. And on and on it goes.

Ah, but I'm setting you up to feel like the victim. Perhaps *you* are
the one who is living behind the wall? Perhaps you are the one who

can only get so close before you feel vulnerable and are forced to retreat to what's comfortable, what's familiar. Maybe you picked up this book hoping to find some answers to why you do what you do. Or maybe someone who loves you left this sitting out in hopes that you would read it, apply it, and thus set the stage for a new level of friendship or perhaps a deeper connection in your marriage. Or maybe you need to break through with one of your children.

Whatever your situation, odds are, you've got some cleaning out to do. We all do. And if you are willing to take what may be a painful look in the mirror, you may find the motivation you need to change. And this book will provide you the tools you need to effect change.

DAMAGED FAITH

On the extreme end of the spectrum, I have met people whose unresolved hurt runs so deep it has erased their faith in God. They no longer believe in a personal God—not for theological reasons, but because they can't get past what happened to them or someone they loved. And if you were to hear their stories, you would understand. If they were to hear *your* story, they would probably understand your dilemma as well. Life can take the legs right out from under our faith.

I've gotten to the point that when I meet somebody who is really down on the church and/or God, I rarely engage them in a theological conversation. Theology is not what drove them to their…theology. Nine times out of ten it was a life experience or a series of experiences that left something misshapen lodged in their hearts. And over time, this something eroded their faith in God. Again, Jesus' words come to mind, "From the heart comes…" and we can fill in the blank.

On many occasions I have seen people's faith spring back to life, seemingly overnight, once they began to address their heart issues. That's exactly what happened with Joe. I met Joe at Starbucks. He was sitting in one of those overstuffed chairs with headphones on and a scowl that said, "Don't anybody come near me." If the expression on his face wasn't enough, Joe was about fifty-five years old and not a small fellow. Everything about his countenance and posture communicated anger. So when I saw him I avoided eye contact and went on about my business.

As I was waiting for my soy latte, Joe approached me and said, "Aren't you Andy?" At that particular moment I wasn't sure if I should be Andy or not. From the look on his face I knew I didn't want to be me. But seeing as there were plenty of people around to witness whatever was about to happen, I nodded.

"Somebody gave me one of your CDs," he said. "I've been listening to it. But I've got to tell you, I have a real problem with God, and the church too, for that matter.

Joe had been through two difficult divorces. His first wife had been sexually abused as a child and was never able to face the issues involved. After thirty years of marriage, the memories of abuse surfaced and eroded their marriage, which ended in divorce. His ex-wife passed away suddenly two years later. Joe then remarried, but after three years this too ended in a heartbreaking divorce. Joe was lonely, a recovering alcoholic. There was no evidence of the existence of God, as far as he could see.

I wasn't sure what to say, so I asked him if he would be willing to read a book. He said he would. I told him to buy Philip Yancey's *Disappointment with God*, but I honestly didn't think he would.

I never expected to see Joe again. But I did.

A couple of weeks later, there he was, sitting in the same chair at Starbucks. This time, no headphones. I remembered his face but not his name. He walked up to me and said, "I read that book." For a minute I couldn't remember what book he was talking about.

Halfway through the conversation I mustered the courage to ask him to remind me of his name. He didn't seem offended. The book hadn't really helped, he said, but it really was a great book.

So I said, "Joe, would you be willing to talk to someone?"

He hesitated. "I don't think it's going to do any good," he said.

I wasn't sure it would either, but I did know that Joe needed help. And I knew just the person who could help him. I got Joe's phone number and connected him with one of our pastors, John Woodall. John called Joe, met him for coffee, and struck up a friendship. That was the last I saw of Joe, for a while.

Three months later I was sitting in that same Starbucks, talking to a student pastor from another church, when in walked Joe. When he saw me he headed straight for my table. The first thing I noticed was that he was smiling. The second thing I noticed was that he was carrying a Bible, a notebook, and a book on marriage.

"I'm getting remarried next week!" he announced. I wasn't sure what to think.

"To who," I asked.

"To Susan!" he exclaimed. Susan was his ex-wife. "Susan and I are getting remarried. John is doing the wedding."

I could see in Joe's eyes that something remarkable had happened. And it had. Over the course of several meetings with John, Joe found the courage to quit blaming and instead take a look at what was rattling around in his heart. He had been an angry man, with reason to be angry. But like so many people, Joe had no idea what to *do about* his anger. And his unresolved anger had eroded his faith to the point where it was almost nonexistent.

John had helped Joe to embrace one of the new habits we will talk about later. And immediately, Joe's faith had come to life. With his renewed faith came the motivation he needed to address other issues in his life. The transformation was so remarkable that Susan noticed and began asking questions. Soon after, she put her faith in Christ. The week before Susan and Joe were remarried, John baptized her in one of our morning services.

Joe's story reminds me of lyrics from the Evanescence tune "Bring Me to Life":

> *How can you see into my eyes like open doors,*
> *Leading you down into my core*
> *Where I've become so numb without a soul,*
> *My spirit sleeping somewhere cold*
> *Until you find it there and lead it back home.*

Like so many, Joe had become numb to the life of God because of damage to his heart. To his credit, Joe had the courage to ask for help. His heavenly Father was eager to respond and brought Joe back to life.

PART II

THE CREATURES WALK AMONG US

Narrator: *The mind of man had thought of everything—except that which was beyond his comprehension!*

IT CAME FROM BENEATH THE SEA (1955)

Joan: *I expected to be frightened on my wedding night, but nothing like this.*

INVASION OF THE SAUCER MEN (1957)

Chapter Five

THE SECRET CHAMBER

Doc: *Anywhere in the galaxy this is a nightmare.*

FORBIDDEN PLANET (1956)

You're unforgiven, so go on living,
  knowing that I've unforgiven you.

THE GO-GO'S, "UNFORGIVEN"

In Hollywood of the 1930s and '40s, Universal Pictures was the undisputed king of the monster movie. Boris Karloff, Bela Lugosi, and Lon Chaney Jr. made their names and careers toiling under heavy makeup on the Universal back lot, thrilling Depression-era audiences in countless horror films. Again and again Universal revived four legendary (and lucrative) screen monsters: Dracula, the Mummy, the Wolf Man, and the Frankenstein Monster.

Later, in the 1950s and '60s and beyond, the Toho Company of Japan mined box office gold by repeatedly reducing the city of Tokyo to rubble with its own brand of movie monster. Rampaging radioactive dinosaurs, alien behemoths, and even prehistoric caterpillars made their home on the stomping grounds around Mount Fuji. Impervious to the weapons of the day, four of these creatures would survive time and again to gain international "prominence": Rodan, Mothra, Ghidorah, and the biggest star of them all, Godzilla.

But long before these terrors roamed the cinematic countryside, another formidable foursome wreaked havoc in the human heart. These four fiends are masters of mayhem, having sent countless thousands fleeing from their homes.

They are the four primary enemies of the heart—four life-blocking agents that become lodged in the heart, poisoning our relationships, our faith, and our character. These corrosive forces gain strength from the darkness. Secrecy is their greatest ally. Left to their own, they grow in power and influence, like a lab experiment gone terribly wrong.

But as we will discover, these creatures lose their power when exposed to light. Like roaches that scatter at the flick of a switch, so these four enemies of the heart dissipate when exposed to the light of truth.

Here they are:

Guilt
Anger
Greed
Jealousy

I shudder to look at them.

Maybe you're wondering why I left *lust* off the list. It's because lust is not a problem to be solved; it is an appetite to be managed—an appetite God created. Now there's a thought! We will talk specifically about lust in a later chapter, but in the meantime here's something to chew on: Lust is actually a *good* thing within the right relationship. Truth be known, if it wasn't for lust, you wouldn't be here.

THE DEBT THAT CAN NEVER BE PAID

Each of the four foes on this list are fueled by a single dynamic, and it is this dynamic that makes each so problematic. Understanding this dynamic is the first step to rendering each of these monsters powerless in your life.

Guilt, anger, greed, jealousy—each results in a debt-to-debtor dynamic that always causes an imbalance in any relationship. If you owe someone money, or vice versa, you know this to be the case. No matter what else is going on at the moment, the debt is always in the room with you. Although the person owed generally has the upper hand in the relationship, the reverse can be true as well. If you've ever been in a situation where

> No matter what else is going on at the moment, the debt is always in the room with you.

someone owed you money and refused to pay, you know that the person owed can feel as powerless and as put upon as a person who is in debt. It all depends upon the personalities (and the arrogance) of those involved. Either way, things are not even. Someone has the upper hand. There is an imbalance.

If we are talking about an overdue debt, one that is unlikely to be paid anytime soon, then the tension rises. Even when everybody in the room is trying to keep a level head and talk about something else entirely, there is a negative vibe that characterizes the interaction.

There are only two ways to resolve this kind of tension: Either somebody has to pay up, or somebody has to cancel the debt. As long as the debt is unpaid or unforgiven, the debt governs the relationship. It becomes a filter for everything.

Now let's take a closer look at the first of the four enemies of the heart.

STOLEN MEMORIES

Guilt says, "I owe you." Guilt is the result of having done something we perceived as wrong. Every wrong we do can be restated as an act of theft, as we'll see in a moment. If I steal from you, I owe you. So the message from a heart laden with guilt is, "I owe!"

For example, consider the man who runs off with another woman and abandons his family. Without realizing it at the time, he has stolen something from every member of his family. He stolen his

**Guilt says,
"I owe you."**

wife's first marriage; he has robbed her of her future, her financial security, her reputation as a wife. From his children's perspective this man has stolen their father and all that a father means to the home. He has robbed them of Christmas, traditions, emotional and financial security, dinners with the family, and so on.

Now the man who did all this doesn't think in terms of what he has taken. Initially, he thinks in terms of what he has gained. But the first time his little girl asks him why he doesn't love Mommy anymore, his heart is stirred. He now feels guilty. Most men in this situation try and—check out these words—"make it up" to their kids. Make *what* up? Make up for what is absent. Make up for what was taken away. But every kid who grows up in this situation knows that there's no way to make up for what was taken by trying to replace it with something else. The only way to make up for Dad not being there to tuck Junior in is for Dad to go home and tuck Junior in.

Dad owes. A debt-to-debtor relationship has been established. And whenever you or I wrong another, we create the same dynamic.

We've even adopted specific terminology for resolving our guilt. We say, "I *owe* her an apology." Why do we "owe" people an apology? Because our hearts tell us we took something, that we're now debtors in some fashion. Consequently, the only way to make things right is to pay up. Even if our only available currency is words—"I'm sorry"—still we feel obligated to pay *something*.

Nothing less than paying that debt will relieve a guilty heart of its burden of guilt. People try to work it off, serve it off, give it off, and even pray it off. But no amount of good deeds, community service, charitable giving, or Sundays in a pew can relieve the guilt. It is a debt. And it must be paid or canceled for a guilty heart to experience relief.

Chapter Six

DIARY OF
A MAD MAN

Lt. McPherson: *I wonder if this thing can read minds.*

Eddie: *Well, if it can, it's gonna be real mad when it gets to me.*

THE THING FROM ANOTHER WORLD (1951)

Have you noticed that an angry man can only get so far until he reconciles the way he thinks things ought to be with the way things are?

DON HENLEY, "MY THANKSGIVING"

Guilt says, "I owe you." *Anger*, on the other hand, says, "You owe *me*." We *get* angry when we don't *get* what we want. That's a pretty important idea, and one you may not agree with right off the bat, so I'll say it again: *Anger is the result of not getting something we want.* What we *want* may include what we *deserve*. Because, after all, who doesn't *want* what they think they *deserve*. With me? If not, read it again. This is important—and not necessarily intuitive. (That means it took me a long time to understand it as well.) Maybe an illustration will help.

Donald worked triple overtime in order to convince his boss to consider him for a management slot opening up in the company's southeastern division. At the time he and his wife, Carla, were living in the Midwest and they liked it there, but Carla's entire family lived in Atlanta and she was expecting their first child. Landing this promotion had personal as well as professional benefits.

Things looked promising. The director of the southeast division retired, as promised, and Donald's boss assured him that he was in the running for the position. Donald and Carla's friends and family were all praying that it would work out. Then something really odd happened. Donald's boss walked into his office, sat down, and announced that *he* had asked to be assigned to the position in Atlanta. Donald couldn't believe it. His boss had never indicated an interest in moving. Worse, he had been encouraging Donald for months to pursue the opportunity.

Two weeks later a company-wide memo announced the big news: Donald's boss had been selected to run the southeast division. And as you might imagine, Donald was angry. Why? Because he didn't get what he wanted.

"But wait," you object, "that's not a fair characterization! He was mad because he felt he *deserved* the promotion. He was angry because his boss had misled him and set him up for disappointment."

You're right. Donald did think he deserved the job. He also thought he deserved to have his boss shoot straight with him. The point is, he didn't get either one of the things he wanted.

I'm not arguing that Donald shouldn't have been mad. But even in this situation where his anger is seemingly justified, it really boils down to the fact that he didn't get what he wanted.

Think about a time when you were really angry. Isn't it true that the entire situation could have been reduced to this simple idea: You wanted something and you didn't get it. In other words, you didn't get what you were convinced you deserved.

Interpreted: Somebody owed you!

UNCLAIMED FREIGHT

Run this through the abandoned family scenario I described earlier and it becomes even clearer. Chances are, you know one or two people whose father ran off with another woman. And the odds are pretty good that those people have, or have had, some anger issues. And that's to be expected. Something was taken from them. Dad made off with their opportunity to have a "normal" family. He stole the family unit.

A kid (or an adult) coming out of that kind of a situation has every right to be angry; he or she has been ripped off. Somebody owes them. In this case it's their dad. But

> The root of anger is the perception that something has been taken. Something is owed you.

what if Dad convinces the kids that he had to leave because their mom never…blah blah blah…and she always…blah blah blah? Well, then Mom owes them too!

Show me an angry person and I'll show you a hurt person. And I guarantee you that person is hurt because something has been taken. Somebody owes them something. (If nothing else, an apology.) We all know folks whose anger could be verbalized in one of the following ways: "You took my reputation." "You stole my family." "You took the best years of my life." "You stole my first marriage." "You robbed me of my teenage years." "You robbed me of my purity." "You owe me a raise." "You owe me an opportunity to try." "You owe me a second chance." "You owe me affection."

Again, here is the point: The root of anger is the perception that something has been taken. Something is owed you. And now a debt-to-debtor relationship has been established.

ANGRY HEARTS

It's easy to believe that the only remedy for our anger is payback. After all, isn't that how you settle a debt? What other option is there? And even if there was some other way around the debt, that wouldn't be fair. People ought to pay what they owe. To cancel a debt is to let the guilty party off the hook. They need to pay; otherwise they will probably turn right around and hurt someone else.

The irony is that, in most cases, the perceived debt can never be paid. How do you pay your twenty-five-year-old son back for not being there for him from the time he was twelve? It can't be done. I started the paragraph saying it is an *irony*, but actually it's a tragedy. It is tragic because people spend much of their lives waiting for debts to be paid that cannot be paid. The opportunity to make things right is long gone, but the anger remains. And in many cases it intensifies…and spreads.

EPIDEMIC

Anger, like each of the four "viruses" we will discuss, refuses to remain isolated or appropriately focused. If anger is lodged in my heart, then before long, I will come to believe that *everybody* owes me. This is why we characterize certain men and women as "an angry person"—it seems as though they are angry all the time with just about everybody. It's their demeanor. Their wrath is not reserved for an offending party. It isn't really *reserved* for anyone. They are equal opportunity avengers. And the closer you get, the more likely it is that you're going to get dumped on. And when it happens you'll find yourself asking, "What did I do to deserve that?" The answer? You didn't let them have their way. That's all it takes.

But have you ever had dealings with someone who is *extremely* angry? Have you noticed that *nothing* you do pleases them? Even if you let them have their way but you don't let them have their way *exactly* the way they wanted it, you still catch grief. Extremely angry people have already decided you won't get it right before you even try. They can't let you get it right, otherwise they would lose their excuse to stay angry. And they can't let that happen. Sick, you say? Sure it is. But then, anger is a heart disease. People with anger lodged in their hearts are sick, and sick people act sick.

TURN IT AROUND

But there I go again. Writing as if you are the victim—as if you may *know* rather than *be* the person with an angry heart. If you aren't sure which side of the equation you're on, just ask the people closest to you. Just say, "I'm reading this book that has made me curious about whether or not I have anger issues. What do you think?" If you already know what they are going to say (or want to say), then there's probably no sense in asking. Just assume this chapter is for you and keep reading.

If you aren't sure but have a nagging suspicion, go ahead and ask. And as your friends and family respond, listen at two levels. Listen to what they are saying. But more importantly, listen to what you are *feeling*. Chances are, their words will stir your heart. *It is when our hearts are stirred that we become most aware of what they contain.*

Now, if they pause before they answer, chances are that they're afraid to tell you the truth. "Afraid!" you say. "What do they have to be afraid of?" Why not ask them that as well.

But here's the real test. If while they're treading ever so slowly out on what they perceive to be very thin ice, you feel like a volcano is slowly brewing inside you, then you might have a problem. If while they are making their case you feel compelled to interrupt and defend—I'm sorry, *explain* yourself, then that ought to tell you something. If you find yourself wanting to just walk away or even run away, pay attention to that. If you find yourself getting angry at your friend for answering a question *you* asked, then yeah, you more than likely have some anger lodged in your heart.

But don't be discouraged. You have just made an extraordinarily helpful discovery. A discovery that could very well set you on your way toward a healthy heart. Like all four of the internal enemies we'll be looking at in this book, anger gains its strength from secrecy. Exposing it is painful and powerful at the same time. And to be honest, if you discover that you are carrying a heart full of anger, that won't come as a surprise to the people who love you most. They have known for a long time. And chances are, they have been praying that one day you would wake up and see it for yourself.

A STORY TO TELL

If in fact it is you who is suffering from this common malady, I bet you have a story to tell. You may have never shared it with anybody, but I bet you've got one. A compelling one. A story that leaves no room for doubt as to the legitimacy of your anger.

If you're one of those people who has never told your story, stop for a minute and ask yourself "Why?" People bump up against your anger, and you are aware of that. Yet you've never explained where all that energy is coming from. Why?

I would like to offer an insight into your hesitancy to tell your story. It goes back to something I said in the last chapter: These monsters of the heart cannot withstand the light of exposure. For you to tell your story would be to drag it out into the light. You know intuitively that bringing it out into the open would cause it to lose its potency, which means you would lose an excuse to stay angry. Besides, the whole ordeal would be so uncomfortable that it's easier just to keep it to yourself.

If this is your situation, do you realize you may be one story away from a healthy heart? Can you see that by forcing yourself to bring your story to light you may deal your anger a fatal blow?

> These monsters of the heart cannot withstand the light of exposure. For you to tell your story is to drag it out into the light.

I remember having this conversation with a guy who was almost twice my age. He was uncomfortable talking, but I decided I was going to do everything in my power to drag his story out of him. Until that time people had pretty much just written him off as a grumpy old man. But I knew there was something else in there, something that was fueling his anger and discontent. He never would tell me, but he said something I'll never forget—something that provided a major clue as to why he refused to open up. He said, "I don't want to talk about it. Besides, it's silly."

Silly? I have a feeling that a long time ago something small invaded his heart and got lodged there. Something silly. Something insignificant. But it hid there in the dark. And in secrecy it began to grow. Soon the tentacles of whatever it was wrapped themselves around his personality, his demeanor, his entire outlook on life. He was probably smart enough to know that whatever it was that had happened did not justify his temperamental behavior. But now he was embarrassed. So he chose to keep it locked away. And in doing so, he continued to feed the anger, to give it power.

So why don't you tell your story? What are you afraid of? Perhaps you know that telling your story will cause it to lose some of its potency. After all, if somebody heard your tale they might suggest you get over it, let it go. And you know they would be right. But your anger has become part of you. You are comfortable with it. You feel threatened by the very idea of letting it go.

TAKING IT TO THE STREETS

On the other hand you may be the kind of person who tells your story every time you get a chance. You *want* to be understood. You enjoy the sympathy. You've learned that people are willing to cut you a bit more slack once they've heard your tale of woe. You know that your story explains your propensity to overreact, to say things you later regret, to punish people whenever you get the opportunity, to lash out at those who fall short of your expectations. It accounts for your temper, your moodiness, and your unpredictable reactions.

But let's be honest. From your perspective your story not only *explains* your behavior, it *justifies* it. It's a built-in excuse for everything you or others don't like about you. It is your crutch. You know you don't act and react the way you should, but rather than do anything about it you fall back on your story. After all, anybody who was raised the way you were—faced the hardships you faced, lived with the rejection and neglect you experienced, was abandoned at an early age as you were—has every reason—no, *right*—in the world to be the way your are.

You have every right to be the way you are. But do you really want to remain this way?

And that's true. You have every right to be the way you are. But do you really want to remain this way?

Here is a question every angry man and woman needs to consider: How long are you going to allow people you don't even like—people who are no longer in your life, maybe even people who aren't even alive anymore—to control your life? How long?

Seriously, get out your calendar and pick a date. Ridiculous? Silly? What's ridiculous is to continue to allow the people who have hurt you the most to influence your current and future relationships. That's not just silly. That's…sick.

POWER GRAB

Margaret would agree. Margaret was a single mom who spent twenty-two years looking for a soul mate. But by her own admission *she* was the problem. Bottom line, she just didn't trust men. And she had reason not to.

As a college student Margaret had started seeing a counselor to deal with an eating disorder. One afternoon he raped her. Afraid and confused, Margaret didn't report the incident. Then she discovered she was pregnant. At that point she told her parents what had happened. Charges were filed. It was her word against his. Nothing came of it.

Nine months later Margaret delivered a healthy baby girl. Then to everyone's surprise, this brave young lady dropped out of school, choosing the life of a single mom. As you might imagine, baby Sarah was both a source of great joy and a constant reminder of what had happened that fateful afternoon.

When I met Margaret, she was forty-two years old. I had just given a talk on the effects of unresolved anger. She waited until everyone had left the room, then walked over with tears in her eyes and a smile on her face and said, "I just have to thank you."

"For what?" I said.

"In the middle of your talk I realized that for the past twenty-two years, I have allowed the man who hurt me the most, a man I never want to see again, to sabotage all of my relationships with men. I realized as well that I have used what happened to me as an excuse for behavior for which I'm ultimately responsible. That ends today."

Then she told me her story.

When Margaret finished, she took a deep breath and let it out slowly. "Believe it or not, these are tears of joy," she said. "I'm free."

Then she hugged me and walked away.

How did Margaret get free? We will discuss that in detail later. The point is, she made a connection that many angry people never make. Margaret discovered that her *justifiable* feelings gave that man power over her. The anger in her heart was enabling a man she had not seen in years to influence her life. Her rage over what he did to her slithered into every relationship she had had since. When she realized what was going on, the insidious hold her anger had on her, Margaret determined in her heart to resolve it. After all, why give that kind of power to the person who had hurt her most?

DISCARDING THE CRUTCHES

That brings me back to my question. How long are you going to allow the people who have hurt you to control your life? Another year? Another chapter? How long? The reason that question can be so frustrating is that we naively believe we don't have any choice in the matter.

While it is true that you can't undo what's been done, it is equally true that you don't have to let the past control your future. In a few pages I am going to discuss in detail how to dislodge anger from your heart, but that information will not be helpful until you do what Margaret did. You've first got to decide that you *can* be free. Then you've got to quit using your story as an excuse.

The problem is that good excuses rarely collect dust. We use them and use them and use them. You've got to decide to discard your crutches. Remember, your story explains your behavior; it doesn't excuse it. Until you are willing to embrace this simple but annoying truth, you will never flush the anger from its hidden lair in your heart. Besides, justifying your behavior by reciting your story gives ongoing power to the people who hurt you. Why continue giving them that kind of leverage in your life?

A SURPRISE ENDING

There *is* an appropriate way to use your story. Not as an excuse, but as a testimony to God's ability to free you from the past. When you allow Him access to that part of your heart that harbors your anger, something amazing will transpire. Your story will no longer explain your behavior; it will stand in stark contrast to it.

You probably know someone who always seems to have it all together, someone who moves through this world with confidence, grace, and a quiet power. Maybe you assumed this person had an unsullied past, grew up in a healthy family environment, and never hit any bumps along the way. Then you hear his or her story, and it is almost unbelievable. You find yourself thinking, *How could someone who grew up in that kind of painful environment turn out to be so...so...perfect?*

That's what happens when a person quits using his story to justify his anger and instead allows God to do heart surgery.

SOMETHING TO GIVE UP

Perhaps you see your anger as an asset, an ally. You've learned to leverage it in certain situations in order to get your *way*—or, as you like to put it, to get things *accomplished*. You believe your anger makes you strong. You think it makes you a better leader. A more effective disciplinarian. A more successful coach. Granted, your anger probably gives you energy at times, and when harnessed and properly focused, it can be a powerful ally in certain situations. But it doesn't make you more effective or successful. It certainly doesn't make you stronger. In fact, the people who are forced to interact with you see it as a weakness. A sickness.

Like guilt, anger alienates us from other people. More times than we care to admit, the shrapnel of our anger pierces those closest to us, loved ones who are innocent and clueless as to what caused us to detonate in their presence. A heart filled with anger is a heart looking to be paid back. Unfortunately, in most cases, it is our unsuspecting friends and family who are made to pay.

Chapter Seven

THE THIRST THAT COULD NOT BE QUENCHED

Howard: *It's hungry! It has to be fed constantly—or it will reach out its magnetic arm and grab at anything within its reach and kill it. It's monstrous, Stewart, monstrous. It grows bigger and bigger!*

THE MAGNETIC MONSTER (1953)

If dirt were dollars,
I wouldn't worry anymore.

DON HENLEY, "IF DIRT WERE DOLLARS"

Quick review. Guilt says "I owe you." Anger says, "You owe me." The third hideous beast on our list is *greed*.

Greed says, "I owe me."

Bottom line, the greedy people believe they deserve every good thing that comes their way. Not only that, but they believe they deserve every good thing that could *possibly* come their way. Their mantra is, *What's mine is mine because I've earned it—and I've got a lot more coming.* Consequently, it is hard to get a greedy person to part with money or stuff. Why? Because it's theirs. And they are scared.

Like the angry man or woman, greedy people usually have a story to tell. And as with the angry person, this story explains their propensity toward greed. For example, being raised in a home with little or no financial security might explain why a man or woman tends to hold tight to whatever amount of money comes their way. Similarly, it's easy to understand why someone who once lost everything would cling to what they have now.

But greed is a different breed than the other three enemies of the heart we will discuss. Greed disguises itself. In fact, while reading these last couple of paragraphs you may have already had a thought along the lines of, *Here's one issue I don't struggle with.* You may even have been tempted to skip ahead. After all, you may have the occasional angry outburst and you may harbor a few guilty secrets, but you certainly aren't greedy. Right?

SEEING THE INVISIBLE

Now that I think about it, I have never *met* a greedy person. By that I mean I have never known a man or woman who would look me in the eye and admit, "I struggle with greed." What they say is, "I'm careful."

The truth is, we've made it almost impossible to identify greed in our own lives. Unlike anger or guilt, greed hides behind several virtues. Greedy people are savers, and saving is a good thing. Greedy people are often planners, and planning is a good thing. Greedy people want to make sure their financial future is secure, and that's a good thing as well. Right?

Greed is easy to hide—from ourselves. But the people around us know. Because although it may be difficult to spot greed in the mirror, it isn't difficult at all to see in the people around us. In fact, we can identify it almost instantly in someone else:

- Greedy people talk a lot and worry a lot about money.
- Greedy people are not cheerful givers.
- Greedy people are reluctant to share.
- Greedy people are poor losers.
- Greedy people quibble over insignificant sums of money.
- Greedy people talk as if they have just enough to get by.
- Greedy people often create a culture of secrecy around them.
- Greedy people won't let you forget what they have done for you.
- Greedy people are reluctant to express gratitude.
- Greedy people are not content with what they have.
- Greedy people attempt to control people with their money.

Greed knows no socioeconomic boundaries. I've met greedy poor people and greedy rich people. Greed is not a *financial* issue; it is a *heart* issue. Financial gain doesn't make greedy people less greedy. Financial gain or loss doesn't change anything, because greed emanates from the heart.

THE MONSTER IN THE MIRROR

Is this an issue for you? Is it hard for you to give away money? Are you quick to make excuses? Do you ask questions intended to make you look like a careful steward when in fact you are looking for an excuse not to give? When you do give, do you feel like the recipient owes you something in return? In other words, are there always strings attached to your gifts?

If this is a heart issue for you, then I can assure you that your family feels like they're competing with your stuff. At times they will feel like you value your stuff over them. They may feel like they have to beg you for whatever they get out of you financially. They see and feel the strings. They hate bringing up financial issues around you.

Sound familiar? Remind you of any conversations you've had lately?

Consider this warning issued by Jesus himself:

"Watch out! Be on your guard against all kinds of greed; a man's life does not consist in the abundance of his posses- sions." (Luke 12:15)

Be on your guard? Why? Because of the four heart conditions we will discuss, greed is the most subtle of all.

And take special note of this statement: "a man's life does not consist in the abundance of his possessions." For the greedy person, stuff equals life. They have bought into the lie, "My stuff is my life." And so to tamper with or ask for or damage their stuff is…well, it's personally threatening. Their stuff is an extension of who they are.

For the greedy person, stuff equals life.

I know a bit more about this than I would like to admit. In fact, I distinctly remember the first time I was confronted with my greed. I was twenty-seven and working as the student pastor at my dad's church. I wasn't making a lot of money, and if anyone had accused me of being greedy I would have laughed.

The incident took place during our summer camp. As it happened, I was the worship leader for the week, which required me to bring my guitar to camp with me. But I didn't want a bunch of teenagers touching my precious guitar, so I brought two guitars. One I kept on stage and the other one—the nice one, the one that was an extension of me—I kept locked in a case off to the side. Anytime a student asked me if he or she could play my guitar, I would say, "Sure!" And then I would point them to the cheap guitar I left out on stage. Pretty good system. Actually, I saw it as good stewardship: I was protecting an asset God had given me to manage.

About halfway through the week, however, a kid walked up and asked if he could play my *good* guitar. The jig was up; they were onto me. I remember standing there trying to come up with a plausible reason why that wasn't such a good idea. I considered lying and telling him that I left the key to the case in my cabin. Greed will make you do that kind of stuff, you know. But seeing as I was there to teach kids not to lie…I swallowed hard, forced a smile, and said, "Sure."

I carefully lifted my precious guitar out of its case and handed it gingerly to this lanky eighth-grader. He sat down and began playing while I stood right there beside him. After a few minutes I realized how stupid I must look, so I wandered off to another part of the room, pretending to be busy, but all the time keeping my eyes on little Eddie Van Halen and my *good* guitar.

Well, as fate or God or bad luck would have it, somebody ran into the room yelling for the kid to hurry out to do something and he jumped up, leaned my guitar against a railing, and hustled toward the door. As he bounded down the steps from the stage, I watched in horror, helpless, as MY good guitar slowly toppled sideways and crashed to the stage floor.

When I reached it there was a dent in the wood and a scratch about an inch long. I was devastated. My perfect guitar wasn't perfect anymore. I was so mad, I wanted to strangle the kid. And then it hit me: I was far, far more concerned with the condition of my guitar than I was the soul of that young man. My heart was exposed. I was so ashamed of myself. I wasn't just being careful—I had a greed problem. I had placed greater value on a possession than on a person. That's the nature of greed.

Here's the real irony of the story. That kid who was responsible for dinging my guitar grew up to become one of the most sought-after worship leaders in America. Not only that, but he has written some of today's most popular worship songs. His name is Todd Fields.

DRIVING FORCE

Fear is the driving force behind greed. Fear fuels greed. Why didn't I want anybody messing with my good guitar? I was *afraid* of what might happen to it. Greed is supported by an endless cast of *what ifs*. What if it gets scratched? What if it gets lost? What if there's not enough? What if I don't get my fair share? What if she has more? What if the economy collapses?

People with greed lodged in their heart fear that God either can't or won't take care of them. More to the point, they're afraid that God won't take care of them in the fashion or style in which they *want* to be cared for. And the gap between what they suspect God might be willing to do and what they want becomes a major source of anxiety. So greedy people shoulder the burden to acquire and maintain everything they need to provide the sense of security they desire.

But therein lies the problem: There's never enough. Greedy people can never have enough to satisfy their need to feel secure in light of every conceivable eventuality. There's always another *what if* that drives them to acquire more. Their appetite cannot be satisfied. So they never feel like they have quite enough, which of course is the very thing they fear. Consequently, greedy people are rarely at peace with others and never at peace with themselves. Greed eventually strains their relationships at every level, eroding long-term relationships over stuff that has a use-life of only a few years. The guitar I mentioned earlier? I don't even own it anymore. In fact, I ended up giving it away to a college student whose guitar had been stolen.

Maybe I learned something after all.

Chapter Eight

ATTACK OF THE GREEN-EYED MONSTER

Dr. Cushing: *She will tear up the whole town until she finds Harry.*

Deputy: *And then she'll tear up Harry.*

ATTACK OF THE 50-FOOT WOMAN (1958)

Death and Destruction are never satisfied, and neither are the eyes of man.

PROVERBS 27:20

As we've seen, each of the enemies of the heart we are discussing is energized by the idea that somebody owes something. Guilt says, "I owe you." Anger is fueled by the notion that you owe me. Greed is kept alive by the assumption that I owe me. This fourth heart issue is no different. *Jealousy.* Jealousy says, "*God* owes me."

When we think about jealousy or envy, we immediately think of the things others have that we lack—looks, skills, opportunities,

health, height, inheritance, etc. We assume that our problem is with
the person who possesses what we lack. But let's face it, God could
have fixed all of that for us. Whatever he gave your neighbor, he
could have given you too. And besides, you don't really want your
neighbor's car; you want one *like* it. You don't mind the fact that God
provided him with one. The problem is that, while passing out new
cars, God skipped you!

The fact that your sister can fit comfortably into a size 3 pair of
jeans is okay with you. The problem is that *you can't*—or shouldn't.
You find yourself staring at her when she's not looking, thinking,
Gee, she looks good…that's disgusting. You know you shouldn't feel this
way, and you try not to let it get in the way of the relationship. You
may even tell your sister how good she looks. But it's always there.
You are continually reminded that she has something you don't. Or
that you have something she doesn't…

The point is, there's an inequity there that God could have remedied.

Let's face it, most of us believe on some level that if God had
taken as good care of us as he has some people we know, our lives
would be richer.

If he hadn't made you quite so wide, you would feel better about
putting on a bathing suit. If he hadn't allowed male-pattern baldness
to strike you down so early in life, poor self-esteem might not be
holding you back. If as a teen you had been as attractive as some of
your classmates, you would have tripled your chances for a date on
Saturday night. If you had been blessed with surpassing athletic ability,
you could have excelled at sports in high school and maybe even
college; that would certainly have changed the trajectory of your life.

If God had made you smarter, you would have done better on the
LSAT and had a shot at law school. If he had gifted you with better

communication skills, you might have worked your way into a top-tier management job by now. If you were a more dynamic public speaker, you might have been given an opportunity to lead a larger church.

What was God thinking?

WHO'S REALLY TO BLAME?

If you are a theist by any definition, your jealousy is really an issue between you and God. What God did for one he could have done for you too. But for some reason he didn't. Your problem isn't with the person who has what you don't; it's with your Creator. *He owes you.*

Yet our jealousy rarely surfaces in our interaction with God. If we're aware of it at all, we might confess it as a sin. But even then we think of our jealousy as an issue between friends, coworkers, or neighbors. It doesn't register as a grudge we are holding against God. But that's exactly what it is.

Instead, it rears its ugly head in our interaction with others. The irony, of course, is that the people we are jealous of can do nothing to remedy the situation. Who has the power to make right the inequity between you and the people who have what you want? Can your brother the all-star make you a better athlete? Can your Harvard-bound sister make you brighter? Can your best friend make you skinnier? Would it really help if your neighbor bought you a car like his? Not really. That would actually make things worse.

GUILTY PLEASURE

Still, the idea of God owing you something probably strikes you the same way it did me at first—absurd. How could God owe *me* something. As a Christian, I've always believed that I owe *him* everything. Perhaps that is why our jealousy is so easily misdirected. And perhaps that is why it seems impossible to conquer. As long as I deceive myself into believing that my problem is with my rich uncle or my skinny sister-in-law, I'll never get to the root of the issue; the tension will never be resolved. Well, almost never.

There is one thing that serves as a salve to my jealousy. It's when the person I envy suffers a setback of some kind. The *only* thing the haves can do to make us have-nots feel better is to lose what they have. Now none of us like to admit this, but there is something satisfying about watching someone you envy lose something you wish you had. We may hate whatever it is in us that secretly rejoices in the loss of another, but it is there.

> As long as I believe that my problem is with my rich uncle or my skinny sister-in-law, I'll never get to the root of my jealousy.

Be honest. Have you ever derived pleasure from watching someone who pulled ahead of you financially suffer a minor setback? Did you feel a twinge of satisfaction when you noticed that your sister-in-law didn't look quite as good at the beach this summer as she did last year? Have you ever taken satisfaction in the ding on your neighbor's car door?

No? Me neither.

But I've heard of people who wrestle with those kinds of thoughts.

Of the four heart invaders under consideration here, perhaps jealousy betrays the true condition of our heart more than any other. I can justify my efforts to conceal my past. I can make a convincing case for my anger. And my greed is easy to camouflage behind the virtues of stewardship and prudence. But how do you justify those incriminating feelings of satisfaction when someone you know (and even love) suffers a setback or loss of some kind? But before you know it, with no conscious effort on your part, there it is: that despicable feeling of *satisfaction*. And where did it come from? Straight from the heart.

NO ONE IS SAFE!

The reason the people you envy can do nothing to remedy your feelings is that *they* are not your problem. Their losses, setbacks, failures, and extra poundage only serve to temporarily alleviate, not eradicate, your pain. Because if it's not them, it will be somebody else. There will always be someone who is richer, skinnier, more talented, better connected, or just plain luckier than you. And until you find a way to deal with your jealous heart, you will be unable to follow the most basic of all Christian tenets—love one another.

As long as jealousy rages unchecked, no relationship you have is safe. Not one. I've seen wives who were so jealous of their husbands they couldn't say *anything* nice about them in public. I've seen fathers who were so jealous of their sons that they couldn't muster a kind word if their lives depended on it. Sports teams, corporate teams, ministry teams—no environment will escape the effects of jealousy. Envy is a powerful force that can wreak irreparable damage upon any relationship or organization. And the irony and tragedy is that the remedy cannot be found by balancing the scales or even by tipping them in the other person's favor. The fact is, somebody's upset with God. And in most cases they don't even know it.

PART III

DESTROY ALL MONSTERS!

General: *When an armed and threatening power lands uninvited in our capitol, we don't meet him with tea and cookies!*

EARTH VS. THE FLYING SAUCERS (1956)

The most powerful agent of growth and transformation is something much more basic than any technique: a change of heart.

JOHN WELWOOD

Chapter Nine

EARTH VS. THE FLYING EXCUSES

Admiral Nelson: *If God ordains that man should die without a fight, then why does he give us the will to live?*

VOYAGE TO THE BOTTOM OF THE SEA (1961)

Maj. Gen. Mann: *Guns, tanks, bombs—they're like toys against them!*

WAR OF THE WORLDS (1953)

Before we go any further we first need to dispel a commonly held myth about *change*. I'm not sure how it got started, but many Christians have embraced this approach to life change which, at the end of the day, leaves many of us wondering if God really has any interest in changing anything, much less our hearts.

To illustrate, let's check in with Brian. Brian has been having trouble getting to sleep at night. He suffers from acid reflux, and lately he has noticed that walking up the single flight of stairs to his bedroom leaves him breathing harder than normal. So Brian makes an appointment to see a cardiologist.

Dr. Plythem runs Brian through an extensive battery of tests, including a grueling three minutes on the treadmill. A week later Brian finds himself in the good doctor's exam room, waiting for the results. The concerned look on Dr. Plythem's face confirms Brian's suspicions: Something isn't right.

Dr. Plythem glances gravely at his chart and says, "On a scale of one to ten, ten being the worst-case scenario, you are a seven. You don't need surgery at this time, but you will if you don't make some immediate lifestyle changes."

"Like what?" Brian asks, a bit worried about what's coming next.

The doctor pulls a single page from his clipboard and hands it to Brian. "This is a three-day-a-week exercise regimen," he explains. "Once your body becomes accustomed to this level of activity, we will bump it up a notch."

"But I don't think you understand," Brian complains. "I can't do all this. I have a bad heart! You said so yourself. Once my heart gets stronger, then yeah, I don't mind exercising. But you can't expect me to do all this stuff in my present condition."

Dr. Plythem looks confused, so Brian continues. "Look, this says you want me to walk for thirty minutes, three times a week. Do you realize how winded I'll be? I'll be sweating like a pig! And if I do these stretches I'll be unbearably sore for days. Doc, I have a bad heart. I can't do all this stuff. Look, first fix my heart, and then I'll seriously consider the routine."

"Brian, I *am* trying to fix your heart. This is how to fix it: by exercising it. The discomfort is part of the cure. You strengthen a muscle by exhausting it and then letting it rest. To fix your heart we've got to exhaust it periodically and then let it rest. And yes, you will sweat. And you will be sore. And you won't always feel too good during the process, but this is the road to recovery."

Brian just shakes his head. "Look, Doc, let me level with you. My wife has been trying to get me to exercise for years. So about a year ago I finally gave in and tried out her treadmill. I wasn't on that thing five minutes before I thought I was going to die. I'm telling you, it won't work. I've already tried exercise. It just made me tired. And there's another thing: Do you know how silly I look in spandex shorts? Like I'm wearing hippo panty hose. Now, once I lose a little weight, I may go for the whole fitness look. But not until then. So if you will please do something to strengthen my heart, then I'll be happy to follow your advice. After all, you're the expert, not me."

At this point Dr. Plythem opens the door and says, "Brian, you're an idiot."

EVERYBODY'S AN IDIOT SOMETIME

I guess a doctor can't really say stuff like that, but I'm sure they all would like to from time to time. And in this particular made-up case, the doctor would be right—Brian is an idiot. You don't wait until your heart is healthy to exercise; you exercise to get and keep your heart in shape.

This is true of the other heart as well. Yet many of us try to use Brian's same line of reasoning with God. And consequently we get the same results.

In churches all over the world people stand together and sing, "Change my heart, oh God, make it ever new; change my heart, oh

God, let me be like you." I wish it were that easy. I wish a changed heart was as simple as singing a song or praying a prayer. Sometimes it is, but in most cases it's not. It requires effort. Sometimes it requires pain. And there's always some discomfort involved. A changed heart is the result of forming some new habits—some exercises for the heart. For that reason most of us would rather sing about it than do the hard work. Like Brian, we want a miracle cure. A quick fix.

But you can't expect to overnight break a bad habit you've spent years behaving yourself into. It takes a habit to break a habit. You can pray every day for a generous heart, but until you start exercising your heart in that direction nothing is going to change. That's like praying, "Lord, give me a smaller appetite and then I'll start eating less." If you want to shrink your appetite, you've got to embark on some appetite-shrinking exercises. You need to develop some new habits.

THAT'S JUST THE WAY I AM

But old habits die hard. Guilt, anger, greed, jealousy—all are habit-forming. And like any habit that goes unchecked, over time they come to define us. These disorders become such a part of us that we no longer view them as issues to be resolved. Instead, we dismiss these destructive habits as characteristics hardwired into our personality.

"That's just the way I am."

"The men in my family are famous for their tempers."

"What can I say? I'm an emotional girl."

"I'm a saver."

Years ago I had a friend, Ralph, who was grossly overweight. When the subject of weight came up, he would smile and say, "I just really enjoy eating." That was his excuse. And Ralph had used that line for so long, he really believed it. From my friend's perspective, he wasn't fat because he lacked self-control; he was simply born with a greater propensity for culinary delectation than the average person. Being fat was part of who he was. His size had nothing to do with habits that needed to be changed. Or so he thought.

But two heart attacks and a couple of bypasses later, my friend dropped the charade and faced reality. It was time for Ralph to elimi-nate some life-threatening habits and embrace a completely different approach to food and exercise.

There's a little bit of Ralph in all of us. We like to laugh off our bad habits as "personality traits." But that doesn't change the truth: They are habits—destructive habits that need to be broken.

And so we pray for change while we make excuses for the very things that need to change. We want to wake up one morning with a generous spirit, guilt-free and anger-free. But when it comes time to do the heavy lifting, doing those habit-

> **You can't expect to overnight break a bad habit you've spent years behaving yourself into.**

breaking exercises necessary to bring about change, something in us resists: *If God wants to change me overnight, fine. But if you're asking me to work at it, then maybe you're trying to make me somebody that I'm not.*

THE TIME IS NOW

In the chapters that follow we are going to look at four specific spiritual exercises that, if you will make them a habit, will effec-tively neutralize the enemies of your heart. Like physical exercise, implementing this regimen is often a matter of sheer discipline. An act of the will. A feeling-defying act of the will. And like physical exercise, these internal "stretches" are always profitable, even when they are not especially enjoyable.

The longer you've been living with guilt, hanging on to anger, clinging to your stuff, or comparing yourself to others, the harder it will be to exercise these four virtues. The longer you have neglected your heart, the harder it is to get it in shape. But in the end it will be worth the effort. I've never met a physically fit person who regretted doing the hard work necessary to get in shape. And I've never met anyone who regretted a good habit. But we all know people who are paying the price for bad habits they never kicked.

In fact, you probably know people who consistently practice the four habits we are about to discuss. You may never have actually seen them engage in these exercises, but there's something about their lives that tips you off to the healthy condition of their hearts. Simply put, they are happy. Genuinely happy. And they are a joy to be around.

HAPPINESS IS A HABIT

When I first started writing this book, I thought about titling it *What Happy People Do to Stay that Way*. We all enter the world on a happiness quest. As a pastor, I would love to believe people are on a *truth* quest, but church attendance figures pretty much quash that theory. What we all want is to be happy. Most of us think we can squeeze it out of somebody or something else, but that never works. Especially for the person being squeezed.

Ask around and you will discover that the happiest people you know are people who have mastered these four habits. Whereas these are learned behaviors, happy people seem to do them instinctively. We tend to think, *Surely she's always been gracious, kind, humble.* But that's rarely the story. Over time these habits have helped to shape this person's character and relationship patterns, often because he or she grew up in an environment where these habits were taught and modeled.

We are tempted to think that happiness is simply a matter of disposition or the product of circumstances. But think about it for a minute. You know people in less-than-enviable circumstances who are genuinely happy. On the other hand, you know people with more stuff than they know what to do with who are never content. Why? Because happiness is not synonymous with wealth. Neither is it synonymous with beauty, marriage, singleness, or any other external circumstance or relational status.

In fact, as we will discover, wealth actually works *against* happiness. Typically, the more a person has, the less generous they are. The more a person has, the more *anxiety* they carry. The more a person has, the more aware they are of what they don't have. I have found that it's actually harder to be happy and rich than happy and not so rich. But don't despair—even the wealthy can master these heart habits. Happiness is no respecter of people. But it *is* the overflow of a healthy heart.

Okay, we've been talking *about* these four habits for eight chapters. Let's confront the first one.

Chapter Ten

THE MEMORY THAT WOULDN'T DIE

Manning: *What kind of sin could a man commit in a single lifetime to bring this upon himself?*

THE AMAZING COLOSSAL MAN (1957)

Jan Compton: *Nothing you can be is more terrible than what I am.*

THE BRAIN THAT WOULDN'T DIE (1962)

E very seasoned vampire slayer knows that a little bit of light is all one needs to separate the good guys from the dead guys. Believe it or not, there is actually a powerful lesson to be learned from Buffy, Van Helsing, and others like them. Secrets, like the walking undead of gothic horror films, lose their power when exposed to light.

Confession exposes our secrets and frees the heart from the oppressive power of guilt. But I'm not talking about the kind of confession most of us are accustomed to—i.e., a simple admission of culpability in a particular incident: "Yes, Mom, I broke your vase." "Yes, honey, I drank out of the milk carton, again." "Yes, officer, that light was red." That kind of confession eases our conscience temporarily but does nothing to expose the deeper secrets we carry. And it is the secrets that keep our hearts in turmoil.

Worse, this kind of confession can actually fuel destructive behavior rather than curb it, leading to more secrets and greater guilt. Let me explain.

One of the first Bible verses I memorized as a child was 1 John 1:9. Watch this—I'll type it from memory:

> If we confess our sins, he is faithful and just to forgive us our sins, and cleanse us from all unrighteousness. (KJV)

This was too good to be true. I mess up, I admit it, God forgives me, I move on. Clearly I had discovered a loophole. Over time this verse became an escape hatch. Every night before I went to sleep, I would carry on an excruciatingly detailed monologue with God. Mostly about my sin. I would try to remember all the sins I had committed that day. Sometimes my list was short; oftentimes it was not. Either way, I was oh so careful to confess each and every thing I had done wrong, thought wrong, and said wrong. And at the end, just to be safe, I would add, "And forgive me for anything I have overlooked."

I went to sleep knowing my sin bucket was empty. But in the back of my mind I knew I would probably fill it up again the next day. In fact, odds were pretty good that I would fill it up with the same sins I had just dumped out before slipping off to sleep. But hey, I confessed! I did what the verse said. And I was counting on God to keep his end of the deal.

But then I began to notice a dangerous trend. When I was tempted to sin, I would reason to myself, *I know this is wrong, but if I go through with it I can always confess it and God will forgive me and everything will be fine.* Before long my confession habit was supporting my sin habit.

It was quite a system I had going.

I'm sure God was wringing his hands and pacing the floor.

After all, I had found a loophole.

EVERYBODY PLAYS

When I got a bit older, I discovered that my Catholic friends had a similar system, but with a slight twist. The way they described it—and keep in mind we were all thirteen at the time—they could do whatever they wanted, then run into confession, lay out all their dirty laundry to a priest, and go on their merry way. I remember thinking, *Do they think God is an idiot?* Surely my friends had to see the hypocrisy in this. In my mind, my Catholic friends were handling confession way different from the way I handled it. But the truth is, there was no real difference at all.

We weren't confessing as a step toward changing. Confession was all about guilt relief. I knew even as I was confessing that I would be back the next day, confessing the same sins. My routine had nothing to do with change. I just wanted to *feel* better.

Chances are, you play your own version of the confession game. Some confess to a priest, some confess directly to God, but none of us is really interested in changing anything. But we sure feel better about ourselves. The cloud lifts. The slate is clean. And now that we've gotten God off our case, we think perhaps he will be on our side. But would *you* side up with someone who treated you that way?

Imagine you had a brother who continually stole from you, embarrassed you publicly, and talked badly about you behind your back—but once a week he came to you and said, in very general terms, he was sorry (which you already knew). But no sooner did you turn around than he was right back at it again. To make matters worse, he has the nerve to ask for your help whenever he gets in a bind. How would you characterize that relationship? Even if you were able to genuinely forgive him each time, what would eventually happen to the relationship? *There would be no relationship.* At best, you would feel used; more than likely, you would feel insulted. *What kind of idiot does he take me for? Does he really think that I believe his apology is sincere when he turns around and does the same things again and again?*

Need I even make the application?

Let's face it, our approach to confession is an insult to our heavenly Father. We certainly wouldn't dream of staying in a relationship with anyone who treated *us* this way. It's a good thing his love is uncondi-tional—otherwise, we would all be in trouble.

Our usual approach to confession is an insult to God.

So where did we go wrong? Why this endless cycle? How is it that we have allowed confes-sion to become a tool that facilitates our sin rather than ending it? Well, I'm glad you asked. Or I'm glad I asked. Anyway, that is a great question and one that deserves consideration.

We play the confession game because somewhere along the way we were taught that the purpose of confession was *conscience relief.* That is, we confess in order to make ourselves feel better about what we have done. And if you want to put a theological spin on it, we confess because we think it will somehow help *God* to feel better about what we have done. According to our twisted way of thinking, confession puts everything back just the way it was before we did whatever it was we did that made us feel like we needed to confess.

But come on, that doesn't even make any sense. How can confessing to God what you did to another person make everything right? How does that restore anything? What about the person you've wronged?

Not only does it not make sense, it doesn't work. This pseudo-confession does not remove our guilt. Like Tylenol, our quick confession prayers take the edge off our pain, but they don't heal the wound caused by our sin. This is why you find yourself repeating and confessing the sins of your past over and over again. The guilt is still there.

THE PURPOSE OF CONFESSION

The English definition of *confession* is to admit to or acknowledge something. But in the Scriptures, confession is associated with *change*. Confession is just one step in a sequence of steps that lead the guilty out of the darkness and into the light; it is simply the beginning of a process that ultimately leads to a change in lifestyle or behavior.

The early Catholic literature on penance and confession support this broadened definition. In the early days of Catholicism, you weren't allowed to confess the same sins over and over. Only once. Because after you did your penance, change was expected. *Penance* comes from the word *repentance*. Repentance is often pictured as a person walking one way, realizing the error of that way, and changing direction to walk in the opposite direction.

In the Scriptures, confession is clearly connected with restitution, repentance, and restoration. In the Old Testament, confession was always public and was associated with *restitution*. Consider this edict from God to Moses:

> "When a man or woman wrongs another in any way and so is unfaithful to the LORD, that person is guilty and must confess the sin he has committed. He must make full restitution for his wrong, add one fifth to it and give it all to the person he has wronged." (Numbers 5:6–7)

For the Jew, this wasn't about feeling better about yourself; it was about making things right with the one you had sinned against—with interest. It wasn't enough to be sorry. God was interested in *change*. And having to go public with your sin and make restitution certainly motivated people to change.

When John the Baptist waded onto the scene, he called people to *repentance* as well as the confession of sins:

> John the Baptist appeared in the wilderness preaching a baptism of repentance for the forgiveness of sins. And all the country of Judea was going out to him, and all the people of Jerusalem; and they were being baptized by him in the Jordan River, *confessing* their sins. (Mark 1:4–5, NASB)

This wasn't private confession. This was public confession made in connection with public repentance. John's audience was going public with their intentions to live a different kind of life. They weren't confessing just to silence their conscience; they were ready to leave their sin behind and head in a different direction. Confession wasn't simply a means to feeling better about their sin; it was a public step toward abandoning sin.

A bit further into the New Testament we find the infamous tax collector Zacchaeus following this Old Testament model of confession. But instead of the required one-fifth that God instituted in the law, Zacchaeus gave back *four times* what he had taken illegally.

Zacchaeus wasn't the cute little man depicted in our childhood songs and Sunday school classes. He was a wicked man considered a traitor to his nation. He had wronged many of his fellow Jews, leaving a trail of relational wreckage in his wake. But when Jesus invited himself over to Zacchaeus's house that fateful day, the little tax collector was changed. He found in Jesus the hope and forgiveness he had long since given up on. But Zacchaeus knew instinctively that it wasn't enough to confess his sins to Jesus. That was a first step, but only a first step.

> "Look, Lord! Here and now I give half of my possessions to the poor, and if I have cheated anybody out of anything, I will pay back four times the amount." (Luke 19:8)

How did Jesus respond? He didn't say, "Oh no, no, no, Zacchaeus! You're forgiven! It was enough that you confessed your sins to me. There's no need to make a public spectacle of yourself." Instead, Jesus said in effect, "Now I know for sure that salvation has come to this house. Your public admission is evidence of a changed heart."

Zacchaeus didn't just admit to his sins of the past, he took public responsibility for them. He confessed in the truest sense of the term.

Over and over the Bible speaks of confession, not in terms of conscience relief, but in terms of life change. Never is confession offered as a substitute for repentance. It is but a first step toward repentance. James, the half-brother of Jesus, had this to say about the role of confession in the life of a believer:

> And the prayer offered in faith will make the sick person well; the Lord will raise him up. If he has sinned, he will be forgiven. Therefore confess your sins to each other and pray for each other so that you may be healed. (James 5:15–16)

James calls for confession to one another as part of our restoration. James seems to indicate here that illness is sometimes caused by hidden sin. Regardless of where you land on that one, don't miss the implication of James's words: Because hidden sin may be the cause of visible illness, the smartest thing you can do is confess. Not only to God, but to other people. In other words, bring out your secrets into the light.

According to this passage, confession precedes physical and spiritual restoration. Again, there is nothing here about relieving your conscience or feeling better about yourself or wiping the slate clean with God. Confession is a first step toward change.

FIRST THINGS FIRST

No doubt this is what Jesus had in mind when he shocked his listeners with this bit of instruction:

"Therefore, if you are offering your gift at the altar and there
remember that your brother has something against you, leave
your gift there in front of the altar. First go and be reconciled
to your brother; then come and offer your gift." (Matthew
5:23–24)

I can imagine someone in Jesus' audience thinking, *Now wait a
minute. You're telling me I've walked all the way to the temple, stood in
line for half the day, and brought an acceptable sacrifice. And I'm supposed to up and leave? You want me to tie up my lamb or hand my pigeon
off to someone else, just to make peace with someone who's mad at me?*

This was certainly a new wrinkle on the Law. Worse than new, it
was terribly inconvenient. And besides, isn't our relationship with God
supposed to be our ultimate priority? Isn't God more interested in our
getting right with him than in getting things right with our next-door
neighbor? Aren't we supposed to put God first? Certainly, we should
be concerned about a strained relationship—but surely it could wait
until after church!

But Jesus comes along
in his characteristic fashion
and reverses everything. In
effect he says our relationship with God hinges on

> **You cannot resolve your
> differences with God if
> you are unwilling to resolve
> your differences with
> the people around you.**

our relationship with other people—the two are inseparable. He
seems to imply that our ability to worship God sincerely and fellowship with him unashamedly is contingent upon the status of our
relationships with others, including those we have offended.

The truth is, you cannot resolve your differences with God if you
are unwilling to resolve your differences with the people around you.

You cannot be in fellowship with the Father and out of fellowship with others over something you have done. The two go hand in hand. Confessing secretly to God or to a priest is no substitute for confessing openly to someone you have wronged. God values relationships and considers restoration a priority. Often, that requires confession—not just to God, but to the offended party.

Part of walking with God is making that call you dread making; setting up that appointment you know will be incredibly awkward; writing that letter that you should have written long ago. It means humbling yourself, owning up to your part of the problem, and doing everything within your power to make those relationships right. And when you swallow your pride and take that extra step, something remarkable happens. Guilt loses its foothold in your heart, and the power of sin is broken in your life.

SOME THINGS NEED TO BE BROKEN

Open confession has the power to break the cycle of sin. Actually, that's the purpose of confession. And like most medicinal remedies, it works when applied properly.

If you start confessing your sins to the people you've sinned against, odds are that you're not going to go back and commit those same sins again. Maybe that's the reason we would rather just confess our sins silently to God—it gives us an out. We can be repeat offenders without embarrassing ourselves. I say "maybe." In fact, that is *exactly* why we confess secretly: In many cases we know we are going to repeat the offense.

But if you force yourself to confess to your sales manager that you inflated your numbers last quarter, assuming you keep your job, you probably aren't going to inflate them again. Not if it means having to confess the same infraction a second time.

If you muster the courage to confess to a friend that you revealed to somebody something she had told you in confidence, chances are you will never do that again. Not if it means having to confess it again.

If you confess to a teacher that you cheated on an exam, that will probably be the last exam you ever cheat on. I know this to be true from personal experience.

Guilty people are usually repeat offenders. And as long as you are carrying a secret, as long as you are trying to ease your conscience by telling God how sorry you are, you are setting yourself up to repeat the past. However, confession—the way God designed confession to be applied—breaks the cycle of sin and guilt. But that's just the beginning.

Chapter Eleven

LURING THEM INTO THE OPEN

Klaatu: *Your choice is simple. Join us and live in peace or pursue your present course and face obliteration. We shall be waiting for your answer.*

The Day the Earth Stood Still (1951)

When our embarrassment level is exceeded by our desperation level we are a candidate for God's grace.

Peter Lord

Public confession has the power to purge our hearts of the guilt that keeps us from living out in the open; secret confession does not.

Several years ago I was preaching for my dad while he was out of town. On that particular Sunday I was talking about the importance of being blameless. I remember saying something like, "If you are truly blameless, then you can stand up to any scrutiny. The president could ask you to take the job of attorney general, and you'd sail through the confirmation hearings without a hitch because your record is clean."

No sooner had these words spilled out of my mouth when suddenly my mind was flooded with the memory of an incident from high school involving me and a family in our church. I was sixteen at the time. I was angry with the father in this particular household because of things he had said about my dad. So I devised a prank that I thought would put the fear of God in the whole family. Fortunately, no one was hurt, but it scared them to death. Especially their youngest daughter.

What I did was wrong. Worse than wrong, it was illegal. Now that I'm a father and a husband, I see the events of that night in a different light. What I did was horrible. If I had been that father, there's probably nothing I wouldn't have done to punish the person who frightened my family in that way.

But they weren't the only ones impacted by the events of that night. I carried the guilt of my crime around with me every day. And no amount of secret confession, prayer, or penance would erase the guilt. I claimed 1 John 1:9 hundreds of times. A few years after the event I even put some cash in their mailbox to pay for the damage I had caused. But even that wouldn't ease the pain.

Finally, I confessed my sin to a pastor in our church. He assured me that I was forgiven and that I needed to move on with my life. I asked him if I should go to the family and confess what I had done. He said, "No." But he was wrong.

Every three or four months or so, I would receive a gentle reminder from the Lord. This time the reminder wasn't all that gentle. Here I was, preaching in my dad's pulpit, and I almost lost my train of thought right in the middle of my message. I remember thinking, *Lord, this is not the time!*

I got through the sermon and went back into my dad's office to have my well-rehearsed conversation with God about this particular incident. I reminded Him that what I had done was in the past, that my sins had been paid for at the cross and I was forgiven. And as usual, the conviction eased but did not completely go away.

A few days later I was having my morning quiet time, and I found I couldn't pray. All I could think about was this incident that had haunted my conscience all this time. For fifteen years I had resisted God over this. But He wouldn't let up. It was as though God was saying, "Andy, you're not blameless. You're hiding something." And I remember thinking, *But it's complicated, and it was so long ago, and it's probably no big deal by now…*

Finally, I concluded that it would be a lot easier to deal with the issue than to continue arguing with God.

So I stood up and got in my car, without the slightest idea what I was going to do. I just had to make things right with this fellow and his family. So I drove to his house. Then I drove past his house. Then I drove past his house again. It took me a long time to get up the nerve to stop. I can't recall another time in my adult life when I've been so nervous about something. I didn't know if he'd be angry, or if he'd just think I was crazy. For all I knew, he would call the police.

Eventually, I parked in the driveway, walked up to the door, and rang the doorbell—and hoped that nobody would answer. The man I had wronged came to the door and greeted me with the most confused look you can imagine. And rightly so. I had never been to his house before. We were never close friends, and I hadn't seen him in years. "Andy? What in the world are you doing way out here? Come on in."

I was dying on the inside. He didn't have a clue why I was there. Which meant he didn't know what I had done. Otherwise, he would have thrown me off his property—or so I thought.

He was alone. By this time his kids were grown and gone.

As soon as I sat down I blurted out, "I've come to apologize." And he just stared at me. He still didn't know. So I said it again. Primarily because I was afraid if I didn't just start, I would lose my nerve. I told him what I had done. And I told him how sorry I was. He just stared at me. If he had stood up and knocked me across the room, I think I would have felt 100 percent better. I certainly deserved it. So I told him that too. Any response from him would be totally justified in my mind. When I finished, he smiled and said, "You know, I had a feeling it was you."

Now, you have to understand, I had carried this for years. And all along, this person had a hunch that I was behind an event that had caused him a great deal of pain and expense. As long as I live, I'll never forget what this gentleman said at the end of our conversation. He looked at me and said, "Andy, this makes me feel good all over."

I saw release in his eyes. He had already forgiven me and said as much. But when I owned up to what I had done, it's as if the healing process was complete. We both had a good cry, and I left. And I was free. The guilt was gone. I had finally confessed.

The reason you still *feel* guilty about things in your past is because they are still unresolved. Telling God you are sorry doesn't resolve your guilt because God was not the only offended party. Talking to God is not enough. Your burden of guilt won't be lifted until you confess to the offended party. Then, and only then, can you live out in the open. Only then will you be free from the secrets that have formed walls between you and the people you love most.

MISPLACED GRACE

"Now wait a minute," you might object, "what about forgiveness? God has forgiven me for my sin. Why do I need to dredge up a bunch of stuff from my past when it's all been paid for at the cross? Besides, I wasn't even a Christian when I did some of those things."

When I hear people make these kind of arguments I have to smile, because I used them myself for years. But when all the theological gymnastics were finished, my guilt remained. Why? Because God was not the only offended party.

Besides, the same Bible that assures us of God's forgiveness also teaches the principle of restitution. Forgiveness does not erase our need to take responsibility for what we have done. In fact, forgiveness should drive our confession.

Part of our confusion in this area stems from a misapplication of the doctrine of grace. When you became a Christian you came face-to-face with the unconditional,

Forgiveness does not erase your need to take responsibility for what you have done.

undeserved grace of God. If you were like me, it was an overwhelming thing to realize that there was nothing you could do to earn your forgiveness or salvation. It was a gift—period. Nothing you did had any merit. Your good deeds did not, and could not, earn you good standing with God.

But that's *not* true of your relationship with others. God has forgiven you, but those you have wronged may not have. In fact, they may very well be held hostage to bitterness and anger over what was done to them. You're kidding yourself if you think that everybody you have wronged has simply forgiven you and gone on with their life. Sure, that's what they ought to do. But if people always did what they "ought to do," forgiveness wouldn't be an issue for us in the first place!

We're kidding ourselves, as well, if we think we're not responsible for making restitution. The grace that was showered on us at salvation did not provide us with an escape hatch from our responsibility to others. On the contrary, that very grace should *compel* us to make restitution to those we've wronged. Christ paid a debt he did not owe and one we could not pay. That kind of love should motivate us to pay those debts we *can* pay to those we *do* owe.

The penalty for our sin, insofar as heaven and hell are concerned, has been dealt with once and for all. The *consequences* of our sins are a different matter altogether. We are avoiding the clear teaching of Scripture if we use our forgiveness as an excuse to avoid the pain and embarrassment of reconciling with others. It is true that you can never repay God for all he's done for you. But you may certainly be able to repay your fellow man for what you have done to him. And doing so is the only way to free your heart from the poison of guilt once and for all.

TURN IT AROUND

If you really want to understand the power of confession, turn it around—put yourself on the receiving end. Think for a moment, whose apology do you most desire and least expect? Who is it that seems completely insensitive to the trouble or hurt they caused you? Imagine how *you* would feel if you got a surprise visit from that person. How would you feel if that individual walked in, sat down, and took full responsibility for what he or she had done? Imagine what might transpire in your heart if, with sincere humility, that person offered to do anything within his or her power to make restitution for what had been taken from you.

My guess is, you would never be the same. It would be almost impossible for you to resist the changes that would begin to take place in your heart. That's the power of confession. Not only does it have the potential to free you from your guilt, but it may also be the path to forgiveness for those you've hurt. Indeed, your words may bring healing to a wounded soul.

Perhaps the greatest consequence of our unwillingness to own up to our responsibility is that it fuels the fires of bitterness and anger in someone else's life. For many who have been hurt and whose souls are filled with self-destructive fury, a simple confession could set them free.

All they need to be released from the eroding forces of bitterness is for the offending party to come and make it right, to say, "I know I could never repay you fully. I know I can't make this go away, but I'm here to let you know that I'm responsible and I am sorry. And I'm willing to do whatever it takes to make it up to you."

For someone out there, you hold the last piece of a puzzle he or she has been attempting to complete for a long time. Owning up to your responsibility may be the thing that allows this man or woman to move on with life. Simply confessing to God does not accomplish that. And confessing to God will not set your heart free from the guilt that is slowly eating away at your character and conscience.

God's forgiveness does not exempt you from the responsibility for confession and restitution. On the contrary, his forgiveness is the very reason to confess. God paid a high price to reconcile you back to him, and now he's calling on you to pay the price to reconcile yourself to others.

GUILT TRIP

At some point in your journey, God is going to call on you to turn and take responsibility for your past. It never fails. Unresolved relationships, debts that have been neglected, apologies never made—these are things God will eventually lead us to own and resolve. How does he do this? Through that nagging, undeniable, irritating sense of guilt that follows you around like a bad cold. You won't be able to confess it away or pray it away.

Sure, it's painful. Yes, it's inconvenient. Embarrassing? Absolutely humiliating at times. But think about this: Your Savior suffered a painful, inconvenient, and terribly humiliating death on a Roman cross for the sake of our past and future sins. They weren't even his own. He took responsibility for the sins of the whole world, and he died so that all men and women could be reconciled to the Father.

In the shadow of the cross, all our excuses amount to nothing.

Let's face it, in the shadow of the cross all our excuses, all our griping, all our rationalization amount to nothing. We really have no excuse. His death was for our good, and his commands regarding confession and reconciliation are for our good as well. He wants you to be completely free from sin's enslavement. Confession enables you to come out from the shadow of sin and into the light where all things are made new.

THE HABIT OF CONFESSION

Confession is not a singular event. It must become a habit of our lives. Like a lot of people I've talked to, I had to learn this the hard way. But once I moved beyond my self-deception, I got busy and cleaned the slate. Not with God, but with the people I had hurt and offended. Since then, confession has become a habit. I keep short accounts. I confess stuff that most people would probably dismiss as irrelevant. But I've seen the damage guilt can cause, and I don't ever want to go there again.

The incident from high school taught me a valuable lesson. Guilt chips away at my self-respect. Confession has the potential to undermine my public respect, but self-respect is far more important. Besides, I can't control what others think of me. I either lose the respect of others or lose respect for myself. Why pollute my heart with guilt in an effort to protect a reputation I may not have anyway?

Remember, the purpose of confession is not to relieve your conscience; it is to effect change and reconciliation. So quit kidding yourself. Break the endless, meaningless confession cycle. Leverage this powerful tool in the way it was intended. Go public with your sin and purge your heart of the guilt that is eroding your confidence and faith.

I have never heard of a man or woman breaking a debilitating habit without public confession. Ask the folks at Alcoholics Anonymous. They will tell you that going public with a habit is the first and possibly the most important step in recovery. Confession breaks the death grip of guilt and sets us free to embrace the future God has for us without dragging around the dead bones of the past.

The consequences of confession are far less severe than the

consequences of concealment. Secrets are like buried splinters: The best thing to do is get it out; otherwise, the wound gets infected. Healing can't begin until the splinter is out—until you confess. Sure it hurts, but you know what? Over time, ignoring the splinter causes you deeper pain and more complications.

So, got any secrets? Are you playing the confession game? Are you relieving your conscience but seeing no change? Ready to break that cycle? Confess. It is a habit that could change everything.

Chapter Twelve

VOYAGE TO THE ANGRY PLANET

Steve (voiceover): *Tokyo, a smoldering memorial to the unknown, an unknown which at this very moment still prevails and could at any time lash out with its terrible destruction anywhere else in the world.*

GODZILLA, KING OF THE MONSTERS (1956)

You keep carrying that anger,
*   it'll eat you up inside.*

DON HENLEY, "HEART OF THE MATTER"

O f the four enemies vying for control of our hearts, this one is the most obvious and perhaps the most dangerous. Anger. When unleashed with unbridled intensity, anger leaves a trail of destruction in its wake. But behind all the huffing and puffing, ranting and raving, brewing and stewing is the most basic of human experiences: We just aren't getting our way.

As we've seen, the angry person approaches life, love, and rela-tionships looking to be paid back. Anger says, "You owe me," and it's often indiscriminate about who is going to be made to pay.

With that in mind, it should come as no surprise to discover that the remedy for anger is *forgiveness*. Whereas guilty people need get in the habit of confessing, angry people need to develop the habit of forgiving. But that's not as easy as it sounds, is it? Perhaps you've tried forgiving, and nothing really changed.

There is much confusion over exactly what it means to forgive. So much so that many of us feel like we're stuck. Whenever I speak on the subject of forgiveness, there always seem to be three kinds of people in the audience: The first group believes they ought to forgive but can't seem to muster the courage to do it; the second group feels they would be letting the offender off the hook, and that doesn't seem right; and the third group claims to have gone through the motions of forgiveness, but those old feelings and memories keep coming back, leaving them to wonder if they've ever really forgiven at all.

So how *do* you forgive someone? How do you know if you have? What if the other person is a repeat offender? What if you don't even know how to get in touch with the offending party? What if you can't stomach the idea of getting in touch with them in the first place? What if they're dead?

AN UNREALISTIC REQUEST

Even though Christ has given us the ultimate example of sacrificial love and forgiveness, the question of what to do with our anger con-tinues to be an issue for his followers. In a letter to the believers in

Ephesus, the apostle Paul makes what appears to be an unreasonable demand:

> Get rid of all bitterness, rage and anger, brawling and slander, along with every form of malice. (Ephesians 4:31)

We are commanded to "get rid of" anger. That doesn't even make any sense, does it? How do you rid yourself of an emotion?

The Greek term translated here as "get rid of" means "to remove; to separate yourself from." Have you ever unintentionally walked through a spider web? You are beboppin' along, humming a tune that just won't go away, and you walk straight into arachnophobia. What do you do? I can tell you what *I* do. I frantically begin to pull at anything and everything that remotely feels like a spider web. Off my face! Out of my hair! Off my clothes! That's the idea that *get rid of* carries. Get it off, and get it off quick.

Did you notice the word "all" in this same verse? Paul lists here every relational wedge he can think of—bitterness, rage, anger, brawling, slander, and just in case he forgot one, he adds "every form of malice." Malice is general ill will toward another person. Paul covers all the bases: Whatever negative emotion you are harboring, regardless of whom you are harboring it against, get rid of it.

This strikes me as incredibly insensitive coming from a guy who lived two thousand years ago and has no idea what's going on in my life. If I, being a total stranger, walked up and demanded that you get rid of all of your bitterness toward your ex-husband or ex-wife or whoever it is that's driving you nuts, what would you think? I could guess, but I probably couldn't get away with putting it in print. The G-rated version would go something like this: "Mind your own business! Besides, you haven't heard my side of the story."

If I stuck around long enough to listen, I would likely discover that you have a pretty convincing case as to why you have every right in the world to be mad and stay mad. By the time you finished with your story, I would probably be tempted to join you in your crusade to pay back whoever it was for whatever they did. You didn't deserve to be treated the way you were treated, and they don't deserve to get away with it.

CONSIDER THE SOURCE

Before we write the apostle Paul off as another pious religious figure who has no idea what's going on in the real world, we should consider that he didn't pen these words while kicked back on a hammock with a laptop on the sandy white beaches of Tahiti. Paul dictated these words from his cell in a Roman prison. Arrested unjustly and extradited to Rome, he had been awaiting trial for more than a year when these words were written. To make matters worse, the political climate in Rome was not favorable to Christians. This new "cult" was viewed with suspicion by the populace as well as the leadership. In spite of these less than ideal circumstances, Paul instructs believers to rid themselves of any traces of bitterness and anger.

But is this even possible? Paul seems to think so. He doesn't qualify his words. He doesn't give anybody an out or point to extreme situations as exceptions. What if he's right? What if there is a way to rid ourselves of our bitterness and anger?

We've already discussed the consequences of walking around with a heart full of anger. Besides, if you struggle with any of the items on Paul's list—bitterness, rage, anger, any form of malice—

then you don't need me to tell you how complicated life can get.

Still, it doesn't sound realistic. After all, your anger is simply a response to the people and events around you. You're just reacting. Right? It's not your fault that your boss is incompetent. Not only is it not your fault, there's nothing you can do about it. And so you drive home in a state of rage every afternoon.

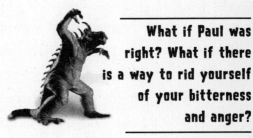

What if Paul was right? What if there is a way to rid yourself of your bitterness and anger?

And it's not your fault that your husband enjoys hanging with the gang at the office more than the gang at home. And there's really nothing you can do about that either. How can you possibly get rid of your anger when your anger is simply a justified response to stuff you have no control over? Bottom line: You are a victim.

Hurt, rejection, criticism, stuff just not going our way—all of these things leave us feeling like victims. No wonder we lash out. No wonder we have such short fuses. Who can blame us? Victims are powerless. Victims have no control over their lives. Victims are at the mercy of others. Victims can only react. Victims are held prisoner by circumstances beyond their control.

It's these feelings of victimization that fuel our justifications and excuses. A victim will always have an excuse. In fact, a victim can write off just about any kind of behavior. After all, look at the way he's been treated. Look at what she's had to endure. What should we expect from someone who has suffered like that? And so pain and hurt create an unassailable wall of excuses and rationalizations.

In time we come to believe the lie: "It's okay for you to behave the way you do. You have no choice. For you, this behavior is perfectly acceptable. You are under no obligation to change. You have every right to be the way you are."

And in the end we have no incentive to change. After all, it's always easier to stay the same and make excuses. Victims don't want to be proactive about changing—they want to be proactive about making sure that the person who hurt them *pays*. And so we spend our energy telling our sad stories rather than taking responsibility for our behavior.

Thus we open the door of our hearts and welcome in the Trojan horse of bitterness. And it stands there, a monument, a constant reminder of a debt someone has yet to pay. Somebody owes us. In time, *everybody* owes us.

So when we read, "Get rid of all bitterness, rage and anger, brawling and slander, along with every form of malice," we think, *There's no way. It's out of my control. I'm just responding to the people and the world around me. I can't get rid of that stuff. Don't ask me.*

THE SECRET FORMULA

So what did Paul know that we don't? What moved him to speak so authoritatively to people whose circumstances he was unfamiliar with? The answer is found in the ensuing passage:

> Get rid of all bitterness, rage and anger, brawling and slander, along with every form of malice. *Be kind and compassionate to one another, forgiving each other…* (Ephesians 4:31–32)

In contrast to bitterness and brawling, Paul suggests that we extend *kindness* and *compassion* to those who have wronged us. And then, with nothing but a comma to separate it out from the rest of the pack, there's our word: "forgiving." The sentence structure here implies that forgiveness is, in fact, the *means* by which we are to do away with our bitterness, rage, and anger—that forgiveness is what enables us to be kind and compassionate to people who have given us neither kindness nor compassion.

If Paul had stopped right there, we could retreat to our well-rehearsed excuses about how badly we've been treated and how unfair life has been. If he had put a period at the end of "other," we could no doubt argue convincingly that the people who fuel our anger don't deserve to

> **Forgiveness enables us to be kind and compassionate to people who have given us neither kindness nor compassion.**

be forgiven. In fact, most of them don't consider themselves in need of forgiveness because they aren't even aware that they've done anything wrong.

But he *didn't* stop there. Paul frames the concept of forgiveness in a way that should cause all of us to pause and reconsider this ancient concept:

> Be kind and compassionate to one another, forgiving each other, *just as in Christ God forgave you.* (Ephesians 4:32)

The kindness and compassion Paul refers to are to be fueled by an attitude of forgiveness. But not just *any* forgiveness. We are to extend an attitude of forgiveness that mirrors the kind God extended toward you in Christ. The little phrase "just as" should be bolded, highlighted, italicized, and doubled in font size. It carries more significance than we will ever understand. "Just as" is what gave

Paul confidence to call people he barely knew to a standard of behavior that most would consider unrealistic. But more importantly, "just as" is the key to allowing God to rid our hearts of the bitterness and resentment that have the potential to reach their destructive tentacles into every important relationship we have. "Just as" redefines and upgrades the meaning of forgiveness.

SETTING LIMITS

Fortunately for us, Jesus tackled the issue of forgiveness head-on during his ministry on earth. Interestingly, it was confusion over this issue of resolving relational conflict that gave Jesus the opportunity to redefine forgiveness for all of us in Matthew 18:21–35.

As a disciple of Christ, Peter understood his responsibility to forgive, but he wasn't sure how far to take it—that is, what do you do about the person who hurts you over and over again. So Peter pulled Jesus aside and asked, "How often shall my brother sin against me and I forgive him? Up to seven times?" (NASB). In other words, *When is enough, enough? How many times do I have to forgive? When is it all right not to forgive?* Peter wanted to do the right thing, but come on, we all have our limits. Where is the justice in a system where forgiveness is offered at every turn?

Peter took a stab at what he believed would be a generous answer: "What about seven times?" Peter was starting to catch on. No doubt, there was a time in Peter's hard-knock life when he would have suggested, "Two times?" or possibly one. But he had been listening. He knew that Jesus' perspective on things was different than that of the religious teachers.

But by asking, "How often shall I forgive?" Peter revealed his own misunderstanding of the nature of forgiveness. Like us, Peter assumed that forgiveness is for the benefit of the offender. And like many of us, Peter was willing to stretch a bit, to be a nice guy: He was willing to go as many as seven rounds with the same person over the same issue. But after that—or some other predetermined point— no more! After all, forgiveness has its limits. Everybody knows that.

Jesus probably smiled, put his hand on Peter's shoulder, and said, "I tell you, not seven, but seventy times seven." And before Peter could respond, Jesus offered one of his most intriguing parables:

> Therefore, the kingdom of heaven is like a king who wanted to settle accounts with his servants. As he began the settlement, a man who owed him ten thousand talents was brought to him. Since he was not able to pay, the master ordered that he and his wife and his children and all that he had be sold to repay the debt. The servant fell on his knees before him. "Be patient with me," he begged, "and I will pay back everything." The servant's master took pity on him, canceled the debt and let him go.

The thing that makes this parable so helpful is that Jesus talks about the emotionally charged topic of forgiveness in terms that everybody can understand. He takes the mystery out of it. Simply put, *forgiveness is the decision to cancel a debt.* This is so simple, so practical, but so easily missed.

Let's back up.

Whenever someone hurts you, there is a sense in which they have taken something from you. A debt is incurred. We touched on this idea in our earlier discussion of guilt. If somebody gossips about you, it amounts to that person stealing your good reputation. When an employer fires a worker unjustly, the employer robs the worker of her financial security. If a man is unfaithful to his wife, he robs her of his emotional security and perhaps much more.

Wherever there is hurt, there is a theft. There is an imbalance. Somebody owes someone. This is why we say things like, "I'm going to get *even* with him." In order to achieve justice, a transaction must take place that transfers something back to the victim. It could be an apology, a favor, money, or some other form of restitution, but the tension will remain until the debt is settled.

Simply put, forgiveness is the decision to cancel a debt.

In Jesus' parable, the master was going to settle his debt with the servant by selling the servant, his wife, his children, and all his possessions—something he had every right to do under ancient law. The servant, on the other hand, did the only thing he could: He pleaded for mercy. Then he did something rather absurd: He promised to pay his debt. Ten thousand talents was an enormous amount of money—more money than the servant would make in his lifetime. His debt was beyond his ability to repay. Fortunately for him, his master was a merciful man. The master took pity on his servant and *canceled his debt*. He decided to forgo his right to be paid back. And *that* is the essence of forgiveness: a decision to cancel a debt.

Jesus continued:

But when that servant went out, he found one of his fellow servants who owed him a hundred denarii. He grabbed him and began to choke him. "Pay back what you owe me!" he demanded. His fellow servant fell to his knees and begged him, "Be patient with me, and I will pay you back."

Now we find the forgiven servant in the same position his master was in—the place of power. His buddy owes him a hundred denarii, a small amount that no doubt his fellow servant could have come up with given a bit of time. And we would expect this man whose massive debt had just been forgiven to extend the same grace to his fellow servant. Instead he "had the man thrown into prison until he could pay the debt." He chose to hold this unfortunate fellow to the original agreement. Worse, he had him thrown in prison until he or a family member could raise the money to pay the debt in full.

When the other servants saw what had happened, they were greatly distressed and went and told their master everything that had happened. Then the master called the servant in. "You wicked servant," he said, "I canceled all that debt of yours…"

There is Jesus' definition of forgiveness: *canceled debt.*

"I canceled all that debt of yours because you begged me to. Shouldn't you have had mercy on your fellow servant just as I had on you?"

To which I'm certain everyone listening to the story nodded vigorously and thought, *Of course he should have had mercy on his fellow servant. Anybody can see that.*

In anger his master turned him over to the jailers...until he should pay back all he owed.

And rightly so! Anybody that ungrateful deserves to have to pay his debt. This wasn't extraordinary punishment; this was simply a matter of holding the servant to his end of the original arrangement. He owed, and he would have to pay. So far, so good.

But the next line, Jesus' closing statement, was the zinger. This was the part of the story nobody expected. If Peter was still wondering what any of this had to do with his original question, it was about to become painfully clear.

Jesus said, "This is how my heavenly Father will treat each of you unless you forgive your brother from your heart."

If the meaning of the parable wasn't clear at the outset, it was certainly clear now. The king in the parable represents God. The servant who had his debts forgiven represents everybody who has had his or her sin debt canceled by God. And wouldn't you know it, the second servant is anybody we are holding something against because of something they have done to us. These are the people who have offended us, hurt us, embarrassed us, abandoned us, or rejected us. These are the people who owe us. The people against whom we have a legitimate case.

And Jesus' words couldn't be any clearer.

Cancel their debt. Forgive them—or else.

What a terrible thing to tell someone who has been taken advantage of! Maybe you're thinking, *Wait a minute! I've already been hurt once. I'm the victim. And now you're telling me that if I don't grant this person forgiveness—which he doesn't deserve—then God's coming after me too? What's up with that?*

GAINING PERSPECTIVE

I've got to be honest here. When Jesus says, "This is how my Father will treat each of you," I don't know with absolute certainty what he's referring to, but obviously, it's not good. Clearly, this was meant as a stern warning to those who refused to forgive. Peter had his answer: *Forgive every time. If you don't, you will pay dearly.* Perhaps Peter saw the irony. Maybe he didn't.

Allow me to summarize: If we hold out waiting to be paid back for the wrongs done to us, *we* will be the ones who pay. If, on the other hand, we cancel the debts owed to us, *we* will be set free.

Our negative reaction to this parable shows our naïveté. From our perspective, we have every right to hold out until we are paid back. From God's perspective, it is possibly the most self-destructive thing we can do.

There may not be a literal prison for those who harbor resentment in their hearts. But we certainly put ourselves in a prison of sorts when we cling to the debts owed to us by others. Perhaps that is what Jesus had in mind when he gave such a stern warning: If *we* demand payment, *we* will pay. His warning is severe because the consequences of ignoring it are severe. Unresolved anger has multi-generational implications.

If your experience with anger is anything like mine, then you know that Jesus' warning is not exaggerated. And it is exactly what we should expect from a Savior who came to earth to rescue us from sin.

Your pain is not a trophy to show off. It is not a story to tell. It is potentially poison to your soul. To refuse to forgive is to choose to self-destruct.

Chapter Thirteen

NOT OF THIS EARTH

Col. Edwards: *This is the most fantastic story I've ever heard.*

Jeff Trent: *And every word of it's true too.*

Col. Edwards: *That's the fantastic part of it.*

<small>PLAN 9 FROM OUTER SPACE (1958)</small>

While we were still sinners, Christ died for us.

<small>ROMANS 5:8</small>

The deeper meaning of the parable of the ungrateful servant probably didn't hit Peter until months later, when he found himself staring at Jesus hanging from a Roman cross. If this was the price of his forgiveness, then who was he to withhold forgiveness from another? God's decision to forgive Peter required the death of his Son; Peter's decision to forgive those who had offended him would cost him little more than his pride.

The same is true for us.

In the shadow of my hurt, forgiveness feels like a decision to reward my enemy. But in the shadow of the cross, forgiveness is merely a gift from one undeserving soul to another. Forgiveness is the gift that ensures my freedom from a prison of bitterness and resentment. When I accept forgiveness from God, I am set free from the penalty of my sin; when I extend forgiveness to my adversary, there is a sense in which I am set free from his sin as well.

This is the force behind the last phrase in Paul's exhortation:

Be kind and compassionate to one another, *forgiving each other, just as in Christ God forgave you*. (Ephesians 4:32)

The kind of forgiveness Paul is talking about doesn't make any sense unless you are a forgiven person. He felt free to command the believers in Ephesus to forgive unconditionally because he was writing to *Christians*—men and women who themselves had experienced the forgiveness of God through Christ.

Whenever I talk to someone who is hesitant to forgive, invariably it's because this person is evaluating his decision in light of what was done *to* him rather than what was done *for* him. There's a big difference. Perspective is everything. As a believer, I am called and liberated to view forgiveness from the perspective of the cross. Like the servant in Jesus' parable, I have been forgiven of a debt I could never repay—the *least* I can do is to cancel the debts owed to us by others. That's what it means to forgive "just as" God forgave me.

If you are a Christian, you are not expected to treat others the way you've been treated by others; you have been called to treat people the way you have been treated by your Father in heaven. You don't forgive because the other person deserves it; you forgive because you have been forgiven.

EVERYDAY OTHERWORLDLINESS

Paul was not talking about a one-time transaction. His present-tense use of the term *forgiving* indicates a mind-set, an attitude, a habit. Forgiveness is a way of life for the man or woman committed to keeping their heart free of anger and bitterness—it's the first line of defense in the face of hurt and disappointment.

In Paul's day there were two different words in the Greek language used to express the concept of forgiveness. The word Paul chose for this admonition conveys the idea of forgiveness as a *gift*. Forgiveness is a gift we are to be constantly giving—like a grandfather who is always ready to dole out quarters to his grandkids, so we are to have forgiveness ready to give on a moment's notice. Specifically, we are called to cancel debts as fast as they are incurred.

> You don't forgive because the other person deserves it; you forgive because *you* have been forgiven.

This does not mean that forgiveness will be something we immediately feel or feel like doing. I don't know that I have ever *felt* like forgiving. Forgiveness runs so contrary to our sense of justice and fairness that it's unlikely we will ever *feel* like forgiving. But in the Scriptures forgiveness is never presented as a feeling; it is always described as a decision. Forgiveness is a gift we decide to give in spite of how we feel.

SLAYING YOUR ANGER

Four phases must take place to complete the cycle of forgiveness. I hesitate to call them "steps." They're more like processes.

1. Identify with whom you are angry.

This may seem kind of silly. But it's not, and here's why. Forgiveness is more than just a decision to move on with your life and forget the past. Trying to *forget* a debt is not the same as *canceling* it. I recommend that you make a list of the people who have mistreated or taken advantage of you. Go back as far as you like, but don't assume you've forgiven someone just because you've "put it behind you."

Whom do you hope to never see again? Whom do you find yourself having imaginary conversations with? Whom would you like to pay back if you thought you could get away with it? Whom do you secretly desire to see fail? Go ahead and poke around every area of your life—family, friends, ex-boyfriend/girlfriend, ex-husband/wife, deceased parent, work associates, coaches, bosses. I know this is no fun, but it is extremely important. This is an opportunity to purge your heart of the junk that has been hindering the relationships you value most. It's worth the effort. Make a list.

2. Determine what they owe you.

This is the step most of us skip. As a result, we forgive generally but not specifically. This is where the parable of the ungrateful servant is so helpful. Just as the king forgave the specific amount owed him by the servant, so we must determine exactly what is owed to us by those who have hurt us.

You know what the person who hurt you *did*, but what exactly did they *take*? Until you know the answer to that question, you are not ready to forgive. Until you know the answer to that question, you may go through the motions of forgiveness but experience no freedom. I've heard it a thousand times: "But I've already forgiven him!" Usually, this is spoken with such intensity that it's obvious forgiveness has not really taken place. *General* forgiveness does not heal *specific* hurts. It is important that you pinpoint what was taken from you.

What do the people on your list owe you? What did they take from you? What would they need to return in order to put things back the way there were? An apology? Money? Time? A marriage? A family? A job? A reputation? An opportunity? A promotion? A chapter of your life?

Be specific.

You cannot cancel a debt that you have not clearly identified.

3. Cancel the debt.

After identifying exactly what was taken, you must cancel the debt. That means deciding that the offending party doesn't owe you anything anymore. Just as Christ canceled your sin debt at Calvary, so you and I must cancel the debts that others have incurred against us. This may be as simple as a decision you make quietly in your heart. Or you may want to mark the decision with something more tangible.

In my father's book *The Gift of Forgiveness*, he tells the story of how he marked the day he forgave his stepfather, John. He actually sat across from an empty chair and spoke as if his stepfather were present. He recounted all the offenses he had held against John through the years and then declared him forgiven. When he finished the "conversation," he stood up, walked away, and was able to leave his anger and resentment behind. Whenever those old feelings began to stir, my father would keep them at bay by reminding himself that those were settled issues. John didn't owe him anymore.

I've heard of people who listed what was owed them, then put the list in an envelope and burned it, and thus declared those debts canceled. I know a lady who buried her list in the backyard. I heard about another fellow who actually nailed his list to a cross as a reminder that Christ had suffered for those sins as well.

There are advantages to physicalizing your decision to forgive. This can be especially helpful for those whose hurt has happened in the past. But for the daily offenses we incur, a quick, simple, but specific declaration is all it takes. Below is an example:

> *Heavenly Father, _____ has taken*
> *_____ from me. I have held on to this debt*
> *long enough. I choose to cancel this debt. _____*
> *doesn't owe me anymore. Just as you forgave me, I*
> *forgive _____ .*

Often I'm asked if it is necessary to tell the person you have forgiven that you have, in fact, forgiven them. In my opinion, no. As a matter of fact, it could do more harm than good. In many cases the offending party doesn't feel as if they've done anything wrong to begin with. Sharing your decision to forgive could be taken as an accusation. The one time when it is *always* appropriate is if someone asks you to forgive them or returns to apologize for an incident from the past. Other than that, this transaction is between you and God.

4. Dismiss the case.

The final process centers on a daily decision not to reopen your case. What makes this so difficult is that our feelings don't automatically follow our decision to forgive. Besides, forgiving someone doesn't erase our memories. If we could forgive and forget, this whole thing would be a lot easier. But in most cases, no sooner have we forgiven than something happens to remind us of the offense all over again. And when our memories are triggered, the old feelings come flooding back.

One of two things usually happens at this juncture. We either (a) take hold of the offense all over again, crank up the imaginary conversations, and reopen our case, or (b) we try not to think about it and turn our thoughts elsewhere. Neither response is appropriate or helpful.

When memories of past hurts flood your mind, *go ahead and face them.* Allow yourself to remember the incident. It's even okay to feel the emotions those memories elicit. But instead of reopening the case against your offender, take this opportunity to restate your decision: "He/she doesn't owe me."

Then thank your heavenly Father for giving you the grace and strength to forgive. Don't accept the lie that you haven't really forgiven. Focus on the truth that this debt has been canceled. How do you know? Because you decided, as an act of your will, to cancel it. Feelings come, feelings go. But the decision remains. He doesn't owe you! She doesn't owe you!

Your memories are not your enemies. Memories are simply memories. What you do with them will determine their impact. Truly forgiving does not always entail truly forgetting.

It's tempting, of course, to judge whether or not you have forgiven by how you *feel* toward your offender. But your feelings toward someone are not an accurate gauge—in fact, your feelings are generally the last thing to come around. But in time, if you cling to the fact that this individual doesn't owe you anymore, your feelings will change. The day will come when you will be able to respond to your offender in light of where he or she stands in relationship to Christ, rather than in light of how that person treated you.

THE FUTILITY OF PAYBACK

The question that begs to be asked in all of this is, "Is it wrong to want to be paid back for what was taken?" The answer is no. There's nothing wrong with wanting to be repaid. The problem is that in most cases it's impossible to be reimbursed for what was taken. Once again, Jesus' parable speaks to our dilemma.

The king who forgave the servant's debt was going to be out a lot of money regardless of how he handled the situation. The servant owed him far more than he would ever be able to repay. Restitution was completely out of the question. Selling the fellow's wife, children, and possessions wouldn't begin to get the king whole. And so it is with us.

To pursue or wait for payback is futile. To insist on it is to set yourself up for unnecessary heartbreak.

Whenever I press people to tell me exactly what was taken by those who hurt them most and what it would take to make things right, they look a bit bewildered. Suddenly they're faced with the realization that they are owed a debt that cannot be paid. Can a man who abandoned his kids ever really replace what he has taken from them? Can a son who has made a parent's life hell for years give back what he has taken? And how do you restore time? Affection? How does a mother pay her grown daughter back for not being there to tuck her in at night as a child? You can't pay back a missing relationship. You can't pay back a reputation. There's no way to make up for years of criticism and neglect. How does someone give you back your innocence? Your purity?

These are debts that cannot be repaid.

The best thing to do is cancel them.

The truth is, nothing can make up for the past. There is an emotional element involved in hurt that cannot be compensated for through apologies, promises, or financial restitution. An apology doesn't erase an experience. To some degree, there will always be an outstanding debt. To pursue or wait for "payback" is futile. It won't happen. It *can't* happen. To insist on it is to set ourselves up for unnecessary heartbreak. To cling to our hurt while waiting to be repaid is to allow the seeds of bitterness to take root and grow. When that happens, we allow the person who hurt us once to hurt us over and over and over again.

THE MORE IMPORTANT QUESTION

It's been my experience that when a person discovers he has heart disease, his overriding concern is not how he got it, where it came from, or whose fault it is that he has it. His number one concern is, "How do I fix it?"

We should be driven by a similar concern when it comes to the anger that pollutes our heart. Blaming won't make us better. Holding out for an apology won't either. The cure is forgiveness. You may need to spend some time dealing with unfinished business from the past. Hopefully, the four processes outlined in this chapter will help facilitate that. But in a world where neglect, insensitivity, and injustice are the norm rather than the exception, forgiveness must become a habit in our lives.

Of the four monstrous forces we will discuss, I believe this one—unresolved anger from intentional and unintentional hurt—is the most devastating. Yet in some ways it is the easiest to overcome. You simply make up your mind to cancel the debt. You decide and declare, "You don't owe me, you don't owe me, you don't owe me anymore. From one forgiven soul to another: You don't owe me."

Chapter Fourteen

INVASION OF THE MONEY SNATCHERS

Gordon Gekko: *Greed, for lack of a better word, is good.*
Greed is right. Greed works. Greed clarifies, cuts through,
and captures the essence of the evolutionary spirit.

WALL STREET (1986)

Frederick: *At last you've got it all, everything I had. Even my*
life. But you're not going to live to enjoy it!

HOUSE ON HAUNTED HILL (1958)

Guilt says, "I owe you." Anger says, "You owe me." Greed says, "*I owe me.*" The person whose heart is coated with greed believes he has earned the good things that have come his way and, therefore, is determined to control his possessions and wealth the way he sees fit. Greedy people have a supersized sense of ownership.

But unbeknownst to most greedy people, greed is fueled by fear. Once you peel back all the excuses and the endless "But what if…?"

153

scenarios, you discover a heart full of fear. Specifically, this person fears that God either can't or won't take care of him. And if God won't, then who will? So greedy people set out to acquire and maintain everything they need to provide the sense of security they desire. But like all human appetites, the appetite for financial security can never be fully and finally satisfied. There's never enough. So the acquisition and hoarding and self-indulgence continues.

But aren't there one or two verses in Proverbs that encourage us to prepare for the eventualities of life? And there's nothing particularly wrong with acquiring things—such as this book, for example. Right? And therein lies the challenge of identifying this particular enemy of the heart. As we've said, this malefactor is able to camouflage itself as a virtue. Greedy people are often savers, and saving is a smart thing to do. Greedy people don't want their children to feel the financial burden of caring for them when they're older, and there's certainly nothing wrong with that.

Perhaps Gordon Gekko was right after all.

Maybe greed *is* good.

Then again…

BIGGER BARN SYNDROME (BBS)

Gordon wasn't the first to editorialize on the topic of greed. Jesus also had something to say on the subject: "Watch out! Be on your guard against all kinds of greed."

Do you want to guess why Jesus began his discourse on greed in Luke 12:15–21 with a warning? He knew back then what we are just beginning to discover: Greed can take up residence in the heart and live there for years, undetected. The unguarded heart is highly susceptible to this debilitating disease. It is difficult to diagnose—especially to self-diagnose.

Jesus goes on to uncover the lie that fuels all greed: "A man's life does not consist in the abundance of his possessions." But doesn't everybody know that? Does anybody really believe that their life is equivalent to what they own? The answer is no and yes. No, not everybody knows that. And yes, there

> **Greed can take up residence in the heart and live there for years, undetected.**

are people who believe that your life is pretty much the sum total of what you own. And many of us today are more prone to this belief than we might imagine.

From here, Jesus launches into a parable about a wealthy landowner whose property yielded a much larger crop than he expected or needed. His good fortune has left him with a dilemma: He has no place to store this bountiful harvest. He thinks to himself, *What shall I do? I have no place to store my crops.* In other words, *What am I going to do with all my stuff that I have as a result of all my hard work?* The landowner has no place to "store" his crops—that's farmer-talk for "save." What he needs is a place to "hoard" his reserves.

In an agricultural society it would be immediately obvious that the abundance of this man's harvest had little to do with his hard work; farmers are always at the mercy of factors over which they have no control. But the greedy man or woman doesn't see the world that way—what comes their way does so because they have *earned* it. And since this landowner believes he has earned this abundance, he never considers the notion that God might have had anything to do with it. And even if he had credited this bounty as God's blessing, it never crosses the landowner's mind that the extra he has been blessed with is intended for anyone's consumption but his own.

Clearly, God had provided this fellow with extra. The question he should be asking is, "Lord, what do you want me to do with the extra?" Just for kicks, I would like for you to say this out loud. Ready? "Lord, what do you want me to do with my extra?" Try it again.

But that's not how greedy people think. And to be honest, that's not how I think either. What about you? When I come into a little extra, I think, *Lucky me!* Like the landowner in the parable, I can always come up with a plan for the extra. And I generally assume it is meant for me. After all, I earned it; therefore, I deserve it. So I store it. Which is exactly what the landowner decides to do:

> Then he said, "This is what I'll do. I will tear down my barns and build bigger ones, and there I will store all my grain and my goods. And I'll say to myself, 'You have plenty of good things laid up for many years. Take life easy; eat, drink and be merry.'"

Bigger barns! What a great idea! That will solve everything; he'll be set for life.

The landowner in this parable is suffering from BBS—*Bigger Barn Syndrome*. BBS is a malady common to those whose hearts are damaged by greed. Come to think of it, my father-in-law actually makes a living from people with BBS. He owns hundreds of miniwarehouses in middle Georgia. They're full of the stuff that people can't fit in their homes. Junk, mostly. But junk that could have been liquidated when it was worth something. Junk that could have been turned into cash that, in turn, could have been put to good use on behalf of someone who didn't have enough. But no, these folks decided to rent a bigger barn. You know why? Because someday, one day, they might need that stuff. So just in case they someday perhaps might possibly need it, they have decided to store—hoard—it.

The good news is, my father-in-law is a very generous man. So every month he collects rent for housing his customers' just-in-case junk and uses a portion of the money to fund worthwhile endeavors. He gets credit for his good stewardship while his customers pay rent on their "stuff." Kind of ironic. So if you live in middle Georgia and suffer from BBS, give Bob a call. He will put your money to good use, even if you are afraid to. Now back to our story...

After declaring his intention to build bigger barns, the landowner offers an explanation as to why he has chosen to pursue this course of action. Keep in mind, greed is always looking for something "good" to hide behind. For instance, this man has decided to build bigger barns to secure his future. Now he will have all he needs for "many years" to come. Nothing wrong with that. Thanks to disciplined planning and opportunistic saving, his kids won't have to take care of him in his old age.

If the story ended there, we might even consider this man a role model. But the story doesn't end there. Nobody's story ends there. While it's true that the landowner planned ahead, he didn't plan far enough ahead. He was right: He *did* need to consider his future—but not in the way he thought. He was presuming on years he didn't have coming to him. Just as he overlooked the God-factor when evaluating his good agricultural fortune, the landowner has overlooked the God-factor when counting how many years he had left.

He assumed that his abundance of stuff assured him an abundance of time. But the two don't have anything to do with each other. The very day the landowner made the decision to keep everything he had earned, he lost it. Or maybe it would be more accurate to say, *it* lost *him*.

Just after this man gets off the phone with the barn-renovation experts, he receives some shocking news: He will die sometime in the night. He is about to learn the hard way that his life is not equivalent to the amount of his possessions. *He will run out of time before he runs out of stuff.*

As it turns out, the landowner is more dependent on God than he realized, for he is entirely reliant on God for his allotment of time. Too bad he didn't see that he was equally dependent on God for his allotment of stuff.

When God delivers the bad news, he asks the landowner a question that is loaded with implication for each of us:

> God said to him, "You fool! This very night your life will be demanded from you. Then who will get what you have prepared for yourself?"

The answer to this question should be obvious: *Someone else.* Someone else will end up with everything he has "earned" and consequently "deserved" and therefore stored up. Someone else will end up with the very stuff he has hoarded for himself instead of depending on God's provision. In the end, all of his possessions will be distributed to others. Not because he is generous, but because he is dead! More irony.

The parable of the rich fool directs our attention to an obvious but often overlooked reality: Eventually, everything we claim to own will be owned by somebody else. In the end it will all be given away. So to assume that everything that comes our way is for our own consumption is shortsighted and foolish. It is not a matter of *if* somebody else will get it; it's just a matter of *when* and *how*. Either we will give it away while we still have time, or it will be taken away when our time runs out.

Jesus closes his parable with a stern warning: "This is how it will be with anyone who stores up things for himself but is not rich toward God."

This is Jesus' definition of a greedy person: A person who stores up things for himself but is not rich toward God. Being "rich toward God" is Jesus-talk for being generous toward those in need. A greedy person is the man or woman who saves carefully but gives sparingly.

> Either you will give it away while you still have time, or it will be taken away when your time runs out.

But what is the warning Jesus is trying to convey? What is he saying will happen to you and me if we are generous savers but not generous givers? Death? I don't think so. That's pretty much a given. Unexpected death? I don't think that's it either. I know a few generous people who died unexpectedly. Conversely, there are some *very old* greedy people; to the chagrin of their greedy relatives, they just keep right on living.

A TOTAL LOSS

The real moral of the story is this: *Those whose eagerness to store up material goods outpaces their willingness to give will suffer a complete and total loss when their time runs out.* The landowner suffered a total reversal of fortune at death: He lost everything in this life and had nothing to show for it in the next. He didn't just lose his life, he lost everything he considered "life." He was rich in this world but poor toward God because everything that came his way was used for his private consumption.

In the words of Jesus, he was a fool. A fool that most of us would have envied had we known him. A fool that many of us have a tendency to emulate, but a fool just the same. The landowner was foolish enough to believe that an abundance of stuff meant an abundance of time. He was a fool to assume that his good fortune was the direct result of his hard work. He was a fool not to give to the less fortunate from his abundance, knowing that the day would come when everything would be taken from him, including any further opportunity to be generous. As Mignon McLaughlin once wrote in *The Second Neurotic's Notebook*, "'Your money or your life.' We know what to do when a burglar makes this demand of us, but not when God does."

The parable of the rich fool does two important things for us: First, it defines greed from God's perspective. Second, it offers a simple remedy. The problem with God's definition is that it's a bit broader than most of us are comfortable with. The problem with his solution is that it is unavoidably practical.

Simply stated, the solution is a habit.

A habit that has the power to free our greed-ridden hearts.

Chapter Fifteen

THE BEAST WITH FIVE STICKY FINGERS

When I have money, I get rid of it quickly, lest it find a way into my heart.

JOHN WESLEY

Maj. Purdue: *It's got to kill us or starve, and we've got to kill it or die.*

IT! THE TERROR FROM BEYOND SPACE (1958)

ere's a question we all need to ask ourselves from time to time: *Why do I have so much?*

Now, I realize you don't have as much as you want. Few of us do. Again, the desire for stuff is like the rest of our appetites—it can never be fully or finally satisfied. But just for a moment, shift your focus away from your *potential* possessions and income and consider your *actual* P&I. Think of all you have. Chances are, it is more than your parents had at your age. Perhaps it is considerably more than most people in the world can lay claim to. So why you? Why do *you* have so much?

We need to slow down occasionally and force ourselves to wrestle with that question. Why? Because a consumer-driven culture keeps us laser-focused on what we *don't have*, and focusing on what we don't have leaves our hearts vulnerable to greed. How? Because as long as I'm on a quest for more, then when more *does* come along I will assume it's all for me. As long as I'm living for the next purchase, the next upgrade, the next whatever, I'm consuming mentally what I hope to soon be consuming physically. I'm anticipating future consumption. That kind of attitude leaves us little margin for generosity. And before we know it, we're building bigger barns or a bigger garage or calling Bob.

So let me ask you again: Why do you have so much? The wealthy landowner believed he deserved it; he didn't recognize the divine providence behind his bumper crop. Assuming you aren't as short-sighted as he was, let me ask the question this way: Why has God provided you with more than you *need*?

If that's an uncomfortable question, consider this: In the past, when you didn't have enough, were you hesitant to question God about your lack? You probably didn't hesitate at all. You let him know immediately that you were in need. And if you're like me, you let him know that you expected *him* to provide for you. And when he came through, what did you do? You thanked him. You may have even shared your story with a few folks. So now that you're on the other side, with more than enough, why don't you question God about that?

When we don't have enough, we wonder why.

Why not wonder when we have more than enough?

THE SURPLUS DILEMMA

You know where I'm going with this. The parable of the rich fool makes it all too clear why we have more than we need. But before we head down the path of predictability, let's consider our options.

What are the possibilities? What might God be up to in providing us with more than our daily bread? Perhaps you have more than you need in order to ensure that your children have everything they need. Is that why God has provided the way he has? Probably not. In fact, leaving or giving your children a lot of money generally does not set them up for success in life. In all my years of counseling I've never heard anyone say, "My problems began when my parents didn't leave me enough money." But the world is *full* of people whose problems began when they received money they didn't earn. I don't think God gave you what you have in order to ruin your kids.

Maybe God provided an abundance for you so you won't worry. Maybe he wants you to lean on your accumulated assets for peace. But I'm guessing that's not it either. Generally speaking, the more a person accumulates, the more they worry about it. Besides, peace is a fruit of the Spirit, not the by-product of accumulated wealth. The more I have, the more I think about it and the more I worry about it.

There's a third option. Perhaps God has provided you with extra in order to elevate your standard of living. Maybe it's all about bumping up your lifestyle a notch or two. After all, that's the American way. In this country we all enter adulthood with the assumption that our *lifestyle* should keep pace with our *income*. In fact, thanks to the credit card industry, for many Americans their lifestyle slightly outpaces their income. Either way, we are continually urged not to allow one to lag too far behind the other. The result, of course, is artificially induced financial pressure.

"Artificial?" you say. "My financial concerns don't feel very artificial." They don't feel artificial because the costs associated with maintaining your lifestyle are very real—you really do have to pay your cable TV bill, your cell phone bill, and your credit card bill. But those bills exist because you have chosen to lead a lifestyle that keeps pace with (or outpaces) your income. You have convinced yourself that all those luxuries are *necessities*—things you can't live without. Your inflated sense of what's essential has created financial pressure, but it is artificial pressure. Maybe all you need to do is throttle back your lifestyle a notch or two and the pressure would subside.

The more I have, the more I think about it and the more I worry about it.

Think about it. Regardless of how much money a person makes, if he leaves himself no margin, there will be no peace of mind. Worse, if all your money is spoken for before you deposit your paycheck, greed has an all-access pass to your heart. Why? Because any extra that comes in is already spoken for as well. You are planning ahead of time to consume it. Where there is no margin financially, there is no way to avoid avarice. When the pressure is on, we have little choice but to think of ourselves first.

That is the essence of greed. You don't have to actually *have* extra to be greedy. As long as you plan to spend whatever comes your way on yourself, you are a candidate. If you have allowed your lifestyle to keep lockstep with or surpass your income, you'll find it is next to impossible to keep greed from taking root in your heart.

EARLY RETIREMENT

Of course, there is one other option to consider. Perhaps God has provided you with extra income so you can retire early. That's what the wealthy landowner in the parable had in mind. But just as it never crossed his mind to be generous with his money, neither did it occur to him to be generous with his time:

> And I'll say to myself, "You have plenty of good things laid
> up for many years. Take life easy; eat, drink and be merry."
> (Luke 12:19)

There are a couple of men serving on our staff who were able to cash out of their companies early thanks to a combination of hard work and good fortune. But instead of heading to Florida to putt their lives away, they decided to plow their leadership and business skills back into the local church. These men were mature enough to recognize that God had not freed up their time just to "eat, drink, and be merry." They understood that their "free" time was a resource to be stewarded responsibly, and so they chose to invest it back into God's kingdom.

There's another fellow in our church who made enough money to retire comfortably in his early forties. He too assumed God wanted him to devote his energies to full-time ministry. But through a series of experiences and conversations, he came to the realization that God had gifted him to make money. *That* was his ministry. So he went back to work, but not to supersize his personal investment portfolio. He returned to work with the goal of funding strategic ministry efforts all over the world.

These men managed to avoid Bigger Barn Syndrome. Like the wealthy landowner, they ended up with more than they needed. But they were wise enough to pause and ask, *Why? Why did God provide me with more than I need?* And in time the answer became clear.

If God is filling up your barns faster than you anticipated, it may be so that he can lead you out of the marketplace earlier than you planned. Now is the time to begin asking *Why? Why do I have more time and resources than I actually need?* In time, the answer will become clear. And when your time eventually runs out, you will have something to show for it in eternity. You will be rich toward God.

CONQUERING GREED

Remember what your mother told you when you had two cookies and your sister had none? "Quick, eat 'em both before she can wrench one out of your greedy little hands!" Probably not. She would say, "Share." What do we tell our own kids, nieces, and nephews when they have more than they need and a friend or sibling has none? We tell them to share. Watching someone eat two cookies in the presence of someone who has none doesn't seem right, does it? We feel compelled to say or do something. Perhaps that is why Jesus said, "Give to the one who asks you, and do not turn away from the one who wants to borrow from you" (Matthew 5:42).

Imagine seeing the world from God's point of view. Imagine being able to see everybody in the world who has two cookies and everybody who has none, all at the same time. You would probably say something. You would tell everyone to share. If God has blessed *you* with more than you need, it is so that you can share your abundance with those who have need. Embracing that simple truth is the key to ridding your heart of greed.

Guilt is conquered with confession.

Anger is conquered with forgiveness.

Greed is conquered with *generosity*.

Generous giving will break the grip of greed on your life. So whether or not you *think* you have extra, give and give generously. You've got to give to the point that it forces you to adjust your lifestyle. If you're not willing to give to the point that it impacts your lifestyle, then according to Jesus you are greedy. If you are consuming to the point of having little or nothing left to give, you are greedy. If you are consuming and saving to the point that there is little or nothing to give, you are greedy.

I know, that's strong. Actually, it's harsh.

But it's true.

Maybe this is a bit hard for you to swallow because you've never had a greedy thought in your life. Maybe you feel compassion every time you see someone in need. And in your heart you really do want to help. You *want* to give, but you can't. Or you won't. Why? Because you are afraid you won't have enough. But your heart genuinely goes out to those in need. So is it fair to say you are greedy? Yes. Because greed is not a feeling; it is a refusal to act.

> **Embracing this simple truth is the key to ridding your heart of greed.**

You can feel compassion toward people in need and be as avaricious as Scrooge. Greed is not evidenced by how you feel but by what you do. Generous feelings and good intentions do not compensate for a greedy heart; in fact, good intentions and greed can cohabit in your heart indefinitely. This is what makes this covert enemy such a threat to the heart. You may never *feel* it the way you do anger or guilt or even jealousy. But it is there. It is dangerous. And it can lead to total loss.

FIRST THINGS FIRST

Just as you can't wait until you're in shape to start exercising, you dare not wait to start giving until your fear of giving is gone. Don't wait until God changes your heart to begin giving. Giving is the way God chooses to change our hearts. As your heart changes, your attitude and feelings will follow suit. God loves a cheerful giver, but he will put your money to good use whether you are cheerful or not. My advice: Give until you get cheerful.

Giving must impact your lifestyle if it is going to break the power of greed.

As I've said, our giving must impact our lifestyle if it is going to break the power of greed. The best way to do that is to become a *percentage giver*. Percentage giving involves giving away a percentage of everything you receive, right off the top, as soon as you get it. Specifically, the first check you would write after depositing your paycheck is a check to an organization(s) that supports the work of the kingdom. That's how you become rich toward God. In New Testament times there were no such organizations; believers gave to their place of worship and to the poor. We now have multiple options. Choose one or two and start. Now.

Writing this check first ensures that God's kingdom gets funded ahead of yours. You'll have to live on the leftovers for a change. If that scares you, start with a low percentage, say 2 percent. You'll never miss it. Bump it up a percentage point every year until you're giving at least 10 or 12 percent of your income. Giving at that level is evidence of a lifestyle adjustment. But percentage giving is just the beginning.

You need to be a spontaneous giver as well. When you see someone in need, give. Isn't that what you expect God to do for you when you are in need? Then go ahead and make the first move. If you've got extra and somebody is in need, share. That's what your extra is there for.

These two habits, percentage giving and spontaneous giving, will protect you from Bigger Barn Syndrome. The day will come when you receive an unexpected windfall and your first thought will be, *Who can I help? What kingdom endeavor can I fund?* In that moment you will know that through the habit of generous giving, you have broken the power of greed in your life.

It is a habit that changes everything.

IT'S NOT UP TO YOU

Before we close this section I want to clarify something: Having money is not a bad thing. It's not knowing *why* you have money that causes problems. Whether you're the beneficiary of hard work, good business sense, savvy investments, a family inheritance, or just plain luck—whatever the case, there's no reason to feel bad about having a lot of money. Besides, it is not really yours anyway.

If we are going to leave it all behind when we die, then one thing is abundantly clear: We are not owners; we are managers. Some people get to manage more than others, but none of us are owners. And as managers, there is never any reason to feel guilty for what we have been given to manage. We shouldn't feel guilty; we should feel responsible. That's what you want your financial adviser to feel, isn't it? Responsible?

I have a friend who manages a portion of my retirement account. I've known him since he was in the sixth grade. I was his youth pastor. I officiated his wedding. We are close. Consequently, he feels very responsible for my money, and he's told me this on several occasions. But he's never told me that he feels guilty. Why should he? I'm the one who asked him to manage it. There's no reason to feel guilty for handling the resources that have been entrusted to you.

The truth is, God owns everything. King David recognized this. For King *Anybody* to acknowledge that God is the owner of everything is unusual. But in David's day, it was generally accepted that the king owned everything and everybody in his realm. But David knew better. He said:

> "Yours, O LORD, is the greatness and the power and the glory and the majesty and the splendor, for everything in heaven and earth is yours. Yours, O LORD, is the kingdom; you are exalted as head over all." (1 Chronicles 29:11)

In my experience, it is the people who haven't come to grips with God's universal ownership who feel guilty about what they have. Managers don't feel guilty. The other thing I've noticed is that people who feel guilty for what they have are rarely responsible with it. Why? Because they believe it's theirs to do with as they please.

When you sit down with a financial planner or money manager, one of the first questions they ask you is, "What are your goals?"

Why? Because they are handling *your* money. The manager's goals are irrelevant at that moment—you aren't discussing *his* money. A good money manager will handle your money with your goals in mind, not his own. If your financial planner received a check from you with no instructions attached, what would be the appropriate thing for him to do? Go shopping? Of course not. A good money manager would call you up and ask, "What do you want me to do with these assets? After all, it is your money."

Come to terms now with the idea that you really are just the manager of Someone else's assets. With this recognition comes a freedom that "owners" never experience. You will be free from the fear of loss in this life—and more concerned with avoiding total loss in the life to come.

Chapter Sixteen

THE INCREDIBLE INSATIABLE APPETITE

Morbius: *You have locked me into hell for eternity. If this is all there is, I would rather die now... I, Morbius, who once led the High Council of the Time Lords, reduced to this—to the condition where I envy a vegetable.*

DOCTOR WHO (1963)

You can't always get what you want.

MICK JAGGER

Time for a quick review.

Every one of the four invaders of the heart is fueled by the notion that somebody owes somebody something. And it is this debt dynamic that gives each of these monsters its power. Regardless of who owes what to whom, as long as someone is holding on to a debt, there will be tension in a relationship.

Guilt says, "I owe you," so the solution is confession. Anger is fueled by the notion that you owe me, so that debt is remedied with forgiveness. Greed is kept alive by the assumption that I owe me— a twisted way of thinking that is remedied through generous giving. The fourth of these insidious threats is similar.

Jealousy says, "*God* owes me."

From the beginning of time, jealousy has played a featured role in the story of human relationships. Cain was jealous of Abel. Esau was jealous of Jacob. Joseph's brothers were jealous of their younger brother's relationship with Dad. Commodus was jealous of Maximus and his relationship with Commodus's father, the emperor of Rome. Woody felt replaced by Buzz.

When we think of jealousy, we think of the things others have that we lack—looks, talent, health, height, money, connections, and so on. And so we think we have a problem with the person who possesses what we lack. But as we've said, God could have fixed all of that. Whatever he's given to your neighbor, he could have chosen to give you as well. Bottom line: If God had taken care of you the way he has some people you know, you would be in much better shape relationally, professionally, and financially.

Your real problem isn't with the people whose stuff you envy; it's with your Creator. God owes you, and you're holding a grudge against him. And until you face up to this simple but oh so convicting truth, jealousy will continue to terrorize your life and wreak havoc in your relationships.

The good news is, this behemoth, like the other three, has a vulnerability. And it's something you might not expect.

But before presenting the solution I want to take a few pages to dissect the problem. Why? Because the driving force behind jealousy is really the driving force behind every single relational struggle you will encounter in your life. Every one of them. From marriage problems to personnel problems in the office, all of them can be reduced down to one common issue. In fact, this issue encompasses and explains the relational rifts caused by guilt, anger, and greed too. Understand this one dynamic and you will be free to quit blaming everything and everybody for less than attractive behaviors that find their source—you guessed it—in your heart.

LOOKING BENEATH THE SURFACE

Now, the notion that every relational conflict can be reduced down to a single underlying problem may strike you as an extreme case of oversimplification. But if you will track with me for the next couple of pages, I think you will agree. Besides, this idea didn't originate with me. Near as I can tell, it originated with a fellow named James, who wrote a bestselling book and whose half-brother turned out to be the Savior of the world. Pretty good credentials.

Anyway, in the fourth chapter of his book, creatively titled *James*, he asks us a question that seems so open-ended it couldn't possibly have just one answer: "What causes fights and quarrels among you?"

Wherever you work, whichever church you attend, whatever kind of dysfunctional family you grew up in, the answer to this question would seem to be as varied as the fights and quarrels themselves. I'm tempted to ask, "Which quarrel are you referring to?" Disagreements and arguments are caused by any number of circumstances, aren't they?

James didn't think so.

He peels back the circumstantial he said/she said excuses and goes right to the heart of the matter—the common denominator for every relational struggle you or I will ever have: "What causes fights and quarrels among you? Don't they come from your desires that battle within you?"

James seemed to think that our external conflicts are the direct result of an internal conflict that has worked its way to the surface. The word "desires" here means pleasures. In fact, this same Greek word is translated "pleasure" later in this passage. James believed that if you and I find ourselves in an argument, it will be because a battle within me has spilled out onto you, and visa versa. According to James, there are conflicting desires churning around inside me, and if you bump me too hard, what's on the inside is going to spill out all over you.

Isn't it interesting that the people we hurt the most are those whom we claim to love the most? The people who birthed us, raised us, exchanged vows with us—why them, of all people? James would say that's simple: They are in close proximity. When I can no longer contain the conflict raging within me, it spills out on those closest to me, even if they're innocent bystanders.

The fact is, the common denominator in all my relational conflicts is ME. The common denominator in all your relational conflicts is YOU.

YOU CAN'T ALWAYS GET WHAT YOU WANT

So what is it that's causing this internal struggle that threatens the peace of every home and office and menaces our every relationship? James comes right out and states it plainly:

You want something but don't get it.

There it is. The source of every conflict you and I will ever experience.

We can't get what we want. We can't have our way.

The term "want" as used here carries the force of *yearn for, lust for,* or *strongly desire*. If you have children then you're very familiar with what James is talking about. When you hear your children arguing, you know instinctively that the real issue is not the toy, the DVD, or who gets to sit in which seat; the real issue is that two people want their way and one is not getting what he or she wants.

James argues that the same is true of every adult conflict. And what do we do? We do whatever we have to do to get what we want…

You want something but don't get it. *You kill and covet*, but you cannot have what you want. (James 4:2)

"Kill" in this verse may be hyperbole, but let's face it, most murders we read about were perpetrated by somebody who wanted something. Even more to the point, most murderers had some kind of personal relationship with their victim. Investigators always begin their investigation with family and so-called friends. Think about it: If you've ever been mad enough to hurt someone, it was because that person didn't give you or someone you loved their due. You weren't getting what you wanted.

James uses another interesting term in this passage: "covet." This word, as used here, means *to hotly pursue* or *to strive after*. The picture is of someone who is constantly trying to meet a need that can't ever seem to be met. But in the end, "you cannot have what you want."

How can James say that? There are times when I get exactly what I want… Don't I? Not really.

James is looking beneath the surface at the *desires* that are constantly swirling around our hearts—hungers that are never fully and finally satisfied. Like my appetite for food, I may feel full after a meal, but three hours later I'm headed back to the kitchen for more. Why? Because an appetite by nature is never fully and finally satisfied; it is only temporarily quelled. No matter how full you feel after a meal, you don't give up eating.

The desires James is referring to in this passage represent unquenchable thirsts—our thirst for stuff, money, recognition, success, progress, intimacy, sex, fun, relationship, partnership. We never get enough of any of these things to fully and finally satisfy our desires. In fact, as C. S. Lewis points out in *Mere Christianity*, the more you feed an appetite, the more it escalates in intensity: "Appetites grow through indulgence—not neglect. Gluttons think just as much about food as starving people."

People with power want more power. Wealthy people want more money. Men and women who bounce from one partner to the next are never fully satisfied with any of them. The point is, our desires and pleasures are not best dealt with by continually trying to satisfy them.

THE FUTILITY OF BLAME

You can see for yourself that our endless, fruitless attempts to satisfy our desires is what fuels our conflicts. Isn't it true that every relational struggle you've ever experienced can be reduced to the other person's trying to satisfy an internal desire in a manner that conflicted with the way you were planning to satisfy your own? And so we quarrel and fight.

When I first considered the significance of this passage in James, I tried rolling it into my repertoire of parenting techniques. Now when I hear my kids arguing, instead of trying to sort out who did what, I first make everybody involved repeat the following: "Do you know what the problem is here? I'm not getting what I want."

My kids hate it. But something very interesting happens: The energy level and volume immediately drop by about half. Most of the time the kids are able to work it out after everyone takes responsibility for what's really going on. And in those instances when I have to drill down further, I find there is almost no defensiveness. They are starting to learn.

The issue in every quarrel is that we each want to get our way. Owning that makes a huge difference. When everybody involved owns it, the problem usually evaporates. James was a pretty smart guy.

> Until I can own my share of the problem, I will always have a tendency to blame the other person.

Until I can own my share of the problem, I will always have a tendency to blame the other person. And blaming never resolved anything. I've never talked to a husband or wife who credited incessant blaming as the source of their marital bliss. Blaming just feeds the problem, but until I can stop and own the fact that my real problem is that I'm not getting what I want, I have no recourse but to blame.

Do you know what blame is? It's an admission that I can't be happy without your cooperation. To blame is to acknowledge dependence: If you don't act a certain way, I can't be satisfied or content. If you take this to its logical extreme, you can never be happy until you are able to control the actions and reactions of everybody you come into contact with—including everybody in your lane and both adjacent lanes on the freeway. And if that's the case, there's no hope!

Until we are willing to fully embrace this truth that James so clearly spells out for us, we have no choice but to try and squeeze our happiness and contentment out of the people around us. The problem is, *they're* trying to squeeze theirs out of *us*. Eventually everybody suffocates. And we walk away convinced that the problem is somebody else. We walk away in search of someone else who can fill us up, fully and finally. And in the busyness and earnestness of our search, we never stop long enough to figure out what it is we really want.

So what is the solution?

THE SOLUTION

What do you do with desires and appetites that can never be fully and finally satisfied? James says you take them to the one who created them in the first place. Now there's a thought.

James writes, "You do not have, because you do not ask God." In other words, we don't get what we want because we're asking the wrong person. Instead of burdening the people we love with desires they were not designed to fulfill in the first place, James instructs us to bring them to our heavenly Father. It's as if God is saying, "By the way, this whole thing could have been avoided

If it's important to you then it's important to God. Because you are important to God.

if you had come to me first instead of trying to squeeze whatever it is you think you need out of the people around you."

Think about it from this angle. Who created those appetites of yours that are never fully and finally filled? Your sister? Your spouse? Your boss? Your neighbor? So why should you expect these mere humans to be capable of satisfying those appetites? James says to take them to God.

Now whenever I suggest this to someone I usually get the same response: "I did that already!" Usually I discover that "I did that already" means "I prayed about it." And "I prayed about it" usually means "I prayed that God would change the heart of _____ , who's not giving me what I think I deserve."

That's not what James is talking about. He's suggesting something far more powerful than asking God to change someone else so that we can get our way. James is instructing us to bring our deepest desires and unmet needs to the Father. He is giving us permission to pour out our hearts in an unfiltered conversation with our Creator.

Peter echoes this sentiment when he writes, "Cast all your anxiety on him because he cares for you" (1 Peter 5:7). In Greek, the term translated "all" means *all*. As in *every*. That means you have been invited to bring every frustration and fear to God. There is nothing too big, nothing too small. You bring 'em all. This means you don't have to begin your prayers with, "I know I shouldn't feel this way, but…" or "I know this may sound petty, but…" or "I know I should be more mature than this, but" or my all-time favorite, "I know that in the grand scheme of things this is really small, but…" None of that is necessary. And here's why: If it's important to you, then it's important to God. Because you are important to God.

Every concern, great and small, matters to the Father because you matter to the Father. Whether it pertains to your love life, your career, your marriage, your parents, your children, your finances, your education, or your appearance, bring it to him. And keep bringing it to him until you find the peace to get up off your knees and face the day confident in the knowledge that he cares for you.

Once you have confessed to him that your root problem is that you're not getting your way, and once you have thoroughly and completely dumped your desires and anxiety on him, you will find it much easier to deal with the people in your life. Regardless of whether they ever give you the recognition, love, or credit you deserve, you will find peace—because you are no longer looking to these people to meet a need that only God can meet.

THE FINE PRINT

When I was in high school, a guy challenged me to memorize the entire book of James. So I did. There's more to the story than that, but the bottom line is, I committed the entire book to memory. Want to hear me recite it? No? Okay.

Anyway, my favorite verse in James was the one we just read: "You do not have, because you do not ask." Back then, I was all about "having." My least favorite verse in the book was the one that followed. To my adolescent way of thinking, it gave God an out. Actually, it *does* give God an out, but I now see that as a good thing. Here's what he says (and I'm writing this from memory):

> When you ask, you do not receive, because you ask with wrong motives, that you may spend what you get on your pleasures. (James 4:3)

That certainly takes all the fun out of it.

James instructs us to bring all of our desires to God but then tells us that God may say no. This was a real disappointment to me at sixteen years old. But if God had given me everything (and everybody) I asked for—for starters, I would have been driving a Porsche 911 to school every day—my life would no doubt have been in tatters within a few years or even months. I'm sure there are a few things you asked God for that in hindsight you're glad he didn't give you. That's because your desires would have ruined you.

The fact is, God loves you too much to give you everything you ask for. He loves the people around you too much to give you everything you ask for. But—and don't miss this—*he still wants you to ask.* He still wants you to bring it all to him.

Why? If there's no guarantee, what's the point?

God wants you to know him as the source of all good things. And when he says no, he wants you to trust him. Actually, it would be easier if God would come out and actually say no. Instead, things just don't change: The Porsche never showed up in the driveway, nobody offered me a record deal, and the L4 and L5 still give me trouble. Like a father who refuses to finance his college-age daughter's party habit and brings her home for a semester, God is not going to finance our self-destructive search for meaning outside of him. He is the source of all *good* things, not all *wished-for* things. But he still wants us to ask, to lean, to depend, to cry out. And he wants us to learn to take no for an answer instead of taking matters into our own hands. That's not always easy, but it is the best option.

THE GOOD AND PERFECT GIFT

James had one more thing to say on this subject:

> Every good and perfect gift is from above, coming down from
> the Father of the heavenly lights, who does not change like
> shifting shadows. (James 1:17)

Every good thing that comes our way comes from our heavenly
Father—which is all the more reason to take our unmet needs, our
heartfelt desires, and even our embarrassing wants and wishes to
him.

At the end of the day, Mick Jagger was right: You can't always get
what you want. Nobody can. It isn't possible. Our appetites can
never be fully and finally satisfied. The question is, are you going to
continue anyway to try and fulfill your desire by wringing it out of
the people around you? Or will you take it to and leave it with your
Father in heaven? These are our only options. One leads to peace,
the other to endless frustration.

Chapter Seventeen

RETURN OF THE GREEN-EYED MONSTER

Envy is the art of counting the other fellow's blessings instead of your own.

HAROLD COFFIN

Lt. Ray Makonnen: *You know, Captain, every year of my life I grow more and more convinced that the wisest and the best is to fix our attention on the good and the beautiful. If you just take the time to look at it.*

THE PHANTOM PLANET (1961)

It is easier for me to own up to my anger than my jealousy. Jealousy always seems so petty. I can build a case for my anger, but as soon as I open my mouth to talk about my feelings of jealousy, I sound a bit middle-schoolish. So I don't talk about it. But I sure feel it. I feel it when I see whose books have become bestsellers ahead of mine. I feel it when I hear someone else preach an incredible sermon. I feel it when I see a guy my age with a head full of thick hair. I feel it when I'm walking down the beach with my tank top on and I see a shirtless guy who has nothing to hide. There are a few other things that stir up feelings of jealousy in me, but that's probably enough self-disclosure for one chapter.

Now that stuff may sound harmless enough, but it isn't.

Jealousy is dangerous. It is dangerous because it shapes our attitudes toward other people. It's hard to actively love someone you're jealous of. It's hard to serve (or submit to) someone who is a constant reminder of what you are not. Eventually, jealousy takes control of our attitudes toward people who have done nothing more than pull ahead of us in a race they are not even aware of. They have excelled in an area we have deemed important, and we hate them for it. Okay, maybe we don't hate them. We just don't enjoy their company. A lot.

Without any real effort on our part, jealousy becomes resentment. But resentment needs justification, so we go looking until we find it. Once we find it, we are safe—there's no need to resolve our feelings because we know that they're perfectly justified. And once jealousy turns to resentment, our jealousy knows no bounds. It has the power to sour our attitudes toward entire categories of people. Rich people, supermodels, bodybuilders, megachurch pastors, stay-at-home moms, career women, big-haired ladies—it's suddenly easy to write off an entire swath of the human race.

Who are you jealous of? Nobody, you say? Maybe.

What about resentment? Here's a question that might bring to light some heretofore—don't you love that word?—some heretofore undiscovered jealousy.

What category of people do you secretly resent?

Dig around a bit. Who really raises your hackles? Professionals?

Performers? Company executives? Marrieds? Singles? Children? Retirees? Look deeper and you will discover that your resentment, with all its shallow justifications, is really a cover for jealousy. And chances are, you'll find that this jealousy began over one incident with one individual somewhere in your past.

CONNECTING THE DOTS

Continue to dig beneath the surface and you will discover that your jealousy is just a manifestation of the fact that you aren't getting what you want. What complicates things is that your dissatisfaction gets reflected off of those around you. But those people are not the source of your problem any more than the moon is a source of light— they're just reflecting back at you what has originated in your heart.

Ridding the heart of jealousy begins with this recognition: *The reason I resent her has nothing to do with her. The problem is that I'm not getting what I want.*

Ridding the heart of jealousy begins with taking a long, hard look in the mirror, not across the street or across the aisle. Focusing our emotion on somebody else fans the flame of jealousy; focusing on our own hearts begins the process of quenching it.

Once you have isolated the problem, the rest is simple. Not easy, but simple. You take your old car, your small house, your hand-me-down dining room table, your forty-inch waist, your eighteen-inch television, your kinky hair, your dead-end job, your poor health, and your less-than-stellar SAT scores to the only one who can do anything about it. And once you get it all gathered up in one big pile of discontentment, you need to pour out your heart to him. All your frustration. All your discontent. Let God know that you know *he could have done better by you.* That's cowboy-talk for, "You could have provided better, given me better opportunities, and while you were at it, upgraded a few of these body parts."

Go ahead and tell him how unhappy you've been with the way he's made you and treated you. He can handle it. Because you are right—he could have done all that. After all, he did it for your sister and your brother-in-law. Heck, look what he's allowed the pagans down the street to own, drive, and look like.

Then summarize it this way.

"Lord, to sum it up: I think you owe me."

Now, if you find it a bit daunting to look God in the eye and accuse him of owing you something, you are on the verge of a breakthrough. If you really do think he has mistreated you and, in fact, *owes* you something, then my suggestion is that you reread the New Testament. Jesus, along with a host of others, makes it pretty clear that we were goners, hopelessly separated from God. But God had mercy and gave us exactly what we did *not* deserve: forgiveness. The price? His Son. The truth is, we owed God a debt we could not pay—so he paid it, thereby erasing forever the possibility of his owing us anything, ever.

Ridding the heart of jealousy begins with taking a long, hard look in the mirror—not across the street or across the aisle.

Our disappointment with not getting what we want or believe we deserve pales in significance next to the fact that we have been given what we most *needed*. In the shadow of the cross, it is clear: God doesn't owe us anything. We owe him *everything*. Including an apology.

An apology for holding him to a debt he doesn't owe—a debt we held against him but failed to recognize in the confusion and whirlwind of emotion that accompanies jealousy.

GOING TO THE SOURCE

At the heart of jealousy is the lie that God owes us. Ridding ourselves of jealousy requires that we face up to and expel this dangerous notion. Having done so, we are free to move unhindered in his direction.

God's unconditional acceptance and grace is the very reason we can bring all our disappointments and dissatisfactions to him with boldness. Again, nothing is too small—we don't have to qualify and explain and feel guilty for how we feel about how we feel. The writer of Hebrews gives us an extraordinary promise in this regard:

> Let us then approach the throne of grace with confidence, so that we may receive mercy and find grace to help us in our time of need. (Hebrews 4:16)

When we come to God with our disappointments and discontentment, we *will* find mercy and grace. Why? The preceding verse explains:

> For we do not have a high priest who is unable to sympathize with our weaknesses, but we have one who has been tempted in every way, just as we are—yet was without sin.

When you bring your wishes and wants, your dreams and disappointments to your heavenly Father, you are bringing them to one who is able to sympathize. You have a Savior who was touched with the same emotions that leave you wondering if you can go on. You can come to his throne unapologetically, boldly, and lay your burden down at the feet of the only one who can do anything about it.

But that's just for starters. Once you have wrestled your jealousy to the mat internally, there is something you can do externally—a new habit—that will keep it in check.

PRACTICALLY SPEAKING

When discussing guilt, we said the antidote was to exercise *confession*. The habit that overcomes anger is *forgiveness*. Greed is overcome by generous *giving*. The habit that will enable you to strengthen your heart against jealousy is *celebration*.

To guard your heart against jealousy, you've got to celebrate the success, size, and stuff of those you have tended to envy. You need to go out of your way to verbally express your congratulations over their accomplishments. This must become a habit. Celebrating the success of those you envy will allow you to conquer those emotions that have the potential to drive a wedge in the relationship.

Author and communicator Louie Giglio is one of my best friends. We've been friends since the sixth grade, when we met under a bunk bed during a shaving cream war at youth camp. We may have met earlier, but this is my first memory of Louie. Throughout high school and college we were inseparable. We preached our first sermons back-to-back on a mission trip the summer after our freshman year in college. After seminary, he went to Baylor University to pursue an additional degree, while I went back to Atlanta to look for a job. Two years later he was speaking to a thousand college students every Monday night, and I was taking junior high kids to Six Flags.

Eventually, Louie and his wife, Shelley, settled back in Atlanta. And fortunately for me, they chose to make North Point their church home. I say fortunately because Louie graciously agrees to do a couple of sermon series every year at North Point.

Now, if you've ever heard Louie speak, you will understand when I say that he is one of the most effective and most sought-after communicators in the

To guard your heart against jealousy, you've got to celebrate the success, size, and stuff of those you tend to envy.

American church. He is uniquely gifted and called. I have never heard anyone take an audience into the presence of God like Louie. I have seen him in front of high school students, and I have heard him speak to college audiences. I've listened to him in a room filled with adults, and I've seen him with church leaders. It doesn't matter who he is speaking to, it's always an incredible experience.

So when I announce to our congregation that Louie will be preaching for the next couple of weeks, people cheer. On the Sundays he speaks, the attendance jumps. And for weeks all I hear is, "Did you hear Louie? He was amazing!" Which, of course, he was.

This makes for a climate fraught with the potential for jealousy.

"Between preachers?!" you gasp. If you only knew.

But in our defense, the potential for professional jealousy is ratcheted up a notch in any profession that involves a performance. And whether or not you like to think of preaching as performing, it is. So preachers are prone to be jealous of one another.

What makes our situation more volatile than most is that in the little town of Alpharetta where we reside there are people who would rather hear Louie than me. Frankly, *I* would rather hear him than me. And there are people who prefer me to Louie. (Primarily my relatives. At least that's what they say to my face.) So people talk and compare and express disappointment when they're expecting to hear one of us and end up with the other. And all of that is natural and normal. But as you can imagine, this creates the potential for some unhealthy competition.

But that's not all. Louie's frequent involvement at North Point has led some to believe that he is on our staff—an associate pastor who fills in when Andy is out of town. In truth, Louie is the founder of his own incredibly successful organization, Choice Resources. In addition, Louie and his team launched the Passion Conferences several years ago. These conferences have been a catalyst for spiritual awakening on college campuses around the world. In addition, he has a record label that serves as the platform for several of the country's premier worship leaders. His scope of ministry far exceeds what I am doing at the local church level. But a lot of people in our town don't know that. To them, he's just the guest speaker.

You get the picture. We are set up for conflict. But there's never been a hint of any of that in our relationship. I'm Louie's biggest fan. I feel like he is mine. And neither of us are shy about how we feel.

Recently, Louie returned from a tour of South Africa where more than nine thousand students flocked to his events. The first time I saw him after he returned, he put his arm around my shoulders and said, "Andy, you wouldn't believe it. Everywhere I went, people were talking about you and the impact of North Point."

What makes this so remarkable is that I know preachers who won't stop talking about all the wonderful things *they* are doing around the world. But that's not Louie. He made it a point to tell me what he discovered about *my* impact, not his. He made it a point to celebrate my success.

I've listened to every sermon Louie has delivered at our church. When I'm in town, I sit on the front row through two and sometimes three services. And yeah, I experience twinges of jealousy over his creativity and insight. And he's a lot "cooler" than I'll ever be. But I'm not about to let any of that drive a wedge in our friendship. So I keep celebrating what God is doing through Louie. And I feel affirmed and celebrated by him as well.

FEELINGS FOLLOW

Perhaps your response to all of this is, "Well, that's just great about you and Louie. Sounds like you have quite the mutual admiration society there in Alpharetta. I'm happy for you. But that's not how I feel about the people around me. Am I supposed to celebrate their success if I don't mean it?"

The short answer is yes. Besides, I'm not asking you to be insincere. Does your sister look good in that dress? If so, tell her. If she doesn't, then you don't have a problem. Do you like your brother-in-law's new car? If so, tell him. If not, then you're off the hook. Did your partner do a good job on that presentation? Did you find yourself wishing it was you? Then tell him he did a good job. You aren't being insincere; you are being honest. However, if he was good and you can't bring yourself to compliment him, now *that's* a problem. If your partner built the house of *your* dreams, tell her. After all, it's true.

Expressing the truth helps to free you from the emotional bondage that is such an integral part of jealousy. When you walk up to the guy who got your promotion and say, "Congratulations," you are refusing to allow dangerous emotions to control your behavior. You are protecting your heart. You are saying "no" to jealousy. It's much easier to behave your way into a new way of thinking than to think your way into a new way of behaving. Don't wait until you feel like celebrating; celebrate until you feel like it. Rid your heart of the destructive forces of jealousy. Refuse to be taken prisoner by emotions that don't reflect reality.

Both of my sons are pitchers on their respective baseball teams. When they come up against a team with superior pitching, it bugs me. I want my son to be better than the kid who's pitching for the other team. When that's not the case, I always make a point of tracking down the other pitcher and telling him what a great job he did. And when I can figure out whose son he is, I congratulate the parents too. It's a habit that keeps my heart free and clear. Reaching out my hand to shake the hand of another father whose son outpitched mine releases all that negative energy and puts everything back into perspective. There's something powerful and liberating about celebrating the success of other people.

Whose success have you been hesitant to celebrate? Who deserves a pat on the back? A letter? A phone call? A hug? Whose progress have you mentally chalked up to luck and therefore refused to acknowledge? Whose achievements have brought to the surface some insecurities in you—insecurities that have caused you to shy away from celebrating their win?

Isn't it time you developed a new habit? Isn't it time you refused to give in to the negative emotions that well up in you when others succeed? Instead of saying nothing or being critical, what if you made it the habit of your life to publicly celebrate the success of others? And when that person's success has the potential to reflect negatively on you, celebrate even harder!

I guarantee you, this is one of those habits that changes everything.

PART IV

WE HAVEN'T SEEN THE LAST OF THEM

The Monitor: *It is indeed typical that you Earth people refuse to believe in the superiority of any world but your own. Children looking into a magnifying glass, imagining the image you see is the image of your true size.*

Dr. Meacham: *Our true size is the size of our God!*

THIS ISLAND EARTH (1955)

Dr. Medford: *We haven't seen the last of them.*

THEM! (1954)

Chapter Eighteen

MONSTERS UNDER THE BED

Dr. Wagner: *But you're sacrificing a human life!*

Dr. Brandon: *Do you cry over a guinea pig?*

Dr. Wagner: *But the boy is so young, the transformation horrible—*

Dr. Brandon: *And you call yourself a scientist! That's why you've never been more than an assistant.*

I WAS A TEENAGE WEREWOLF (1957)

Sometimes I wish I were a little kid again.
  Skinned knees are easier to fix than broken hearts.

AUTHOR UNKNOWN

I have a friend who, from all outward appearances, is a picture of health. He's in great shape. He eats right, exercises, and doesn't smoke or drink. He's never had any heart problems. In spite of all that, he spends half a day every year with his cardiologist, undergoing a rigorous battery of tests. Why? Because his father died of a heart attack in his forties. My buddy was told then that he would always have a propensity towards heart disease. So he keeps a tight reign on his lifestyle, and he sees his doctor regularly. It's certainly not his fault that his heart isn't as strong as the average person's. But regardless, he is responsible for his health.

Then during one particular visit to the cardiologist, as my friend was being wired up for another grueling session on the treadmill, something occurred to him: Just as he was predisposed to heart disease because of heredity, his children would likely be cursed with the same weakness. At the time, his kids were still young. But regardless, my friend suddenly felt another layer of responsibility settle over him as he started his fifteen-minute run to nowhere.

THE HANDOFF

I read somewhere that approximately 50 percent of all heart problems can be attributed to genetics, and about the same percentage to environmental factors. I don't know how those percentages break down when it comes to our spiritual hearts, but I do know that heredity and environment both play a role.

For example, my oldest son, Andrew, processes life exactly as I do. My sister-in-law jokes that her son comes by his overly inquisitive mind honestly—she was the same way as a kid. "Like father, like son" is not just a cliché; there's a lot of truth there. Every once in a while I will respond to something in a way that causes my wife, Sandra, to smile and say, "Is that right, Charles?" (a reference to my dad). I know I have his hands, but apparently I've got more of him in me than I'm aware. And for the most part, that's a good thing. But every once in a while I will hear myself say something and think, *That's something my dad would say.*

Both of my sons are already wearing contact lenses, thanks to me. But what else will they struggle with because of me? And more importantly, what can I do to prepare them for those eventualities? My wife is perfect. I think my daughter may be as well. But what can I do to protect her pure heart? What do I need to teach her to enable her to guard it herself in the future?

Our kids share more than our physical genes. They may also share our propensities towards anger, guilt, greed, and jealousy. Clearly, we have the capacity to pass along the seeds of spiritual corruption, so our children are among the primary reasons *we* need to tackle these issues head-on in our own lives. The fact is, the four heart conditions we've been discussing shape the climate of our homes, which ultimately plays a large role in shaping the hearts of our children.

Guilt has an interesting and potentially harmful way of trickling from the front seat to the backseat of the SUV. A parent with secrets or a secret life will not create an environment of openness in the home. There will always be things that are never talked about. That kid on the Little League baseball team who blows his top when things don't go his way is usually related to the dad in the stands who is prone to go off on the sixteen-year-old umpire. A father with an anger problem will create rage in the hearts of his children through his own incessant overreactions. A mom who is continually talking about what she doesn't have in comparison to others will create that same sense of unhealthy discontentment within her own daughter.

Home environments mirror the hearts of those who head the home. If you can't see this in your current situation, just think back to your family of childhood. You can probably trace some of your current heart-related struggles back to that home environment.

When it comes to shaping our children's hearts, modeling will

Home environments mirror the hearts of those who head the home.

always win out over instruction. I heard a guy at a restaurant yell at his daughter, "Teresa, don't raise your voice to your mother!" I saw the humor in it, but Teresa didn't think it was too funny. She shot right back at him, "I'm not raising my voice!"

Kids raise their voices because they hear us do it. Kids will open up if they see us opening up, even if it means we're opening fire. But our kids will be less defensive if they see us dropping our defenses. They learn to manage their hearts by watching us.

Not long ago I noticed how our kids tend to take responsibility for their mistakes. Saying "I'm sorry" or "That was my fault" comes naturally to them. I commented on this to Sandra. I said, "Have you noticed how quick our kids are to take responsibility when they do something wrong? I don't think I ever said, 'That was my fault' when I was their age."

Sandra smiled and said, "Do you know why it's easy for them to say, 'That was my fault'?" I had no idea. She said, "Because they hear you say it all the time." We both laughed, but she was right. I do say it a lot. And consequently, so do they.

MOVING ON FROM HERE

We cannot control everything our children experience, but we can influence how they process what life sends their way. We can teach them how to guard their hearts against the inevitable firestorms of life. No one impacts the health of a child's heart like Mom and Dad. Intentionally or unintentionally, on purpose or by accident, we build into our children or take away. This may be our greatest responsibility as parents.

Academics are important, but I haven't met too many adults who trace their problems back to where they went to school or what their GPA was. The men and women I've counseled who were teetering on the brink of disaster, relationally or financially, were all dealing with heart problems: Their anger had finally caused irreparable damage to their career; or their greed had taken its toll on their finances; or their jealousy had driven a wedge in their marriage. These men and women had failed to stand watch over their hearts. They were not in the habit of investing in *the* thing that made *the* most difference in *the* most critical components of life.

The question I must wrestle with as a parent is, *When my kids pack their cars and leave home once and for all, what will be packed away in their hearts? And what can I do now to prepare them for the day when their hearts are totally their responsibility?* I am so intentional about so many things involving my kids. Education, sports, music lessons, SAT preparation, even church attendance. Still, I am convinced that at the end of the day they have the potential to be experience-rich yet unprepared for what life will throw at their hearts. If you are a parent, I'm sure you can identify with my concerns.

So what do we do? Other than do all we can to get our own hearts in shape, what can we do to infuse health into the hearts of our children? For starters we can teach them the importance of confession, forgiveness, and generosity. We can teach them to celebrate the successes of others. We can pray. We can model good habits. We can make sure they are in church. We can look for teachable moments. All of those things are important. And when applied consistently, I'm convinced they make a huge difference. But I would like to suggest one other thing that I believe adds a critical element of intentionality to the entire process: It's an exercise that may help our children learn to pay attention to what's going on *within*.

STANDING GUARD

One of the first verses I memorized as a kid was Proverbs 4:23. It wasn't my idea. My dad suggested it. And it proved to be another in a long list of good suggestions. Here it is:

> Watch over your heart with all diligence, for from it flow the springs of life. (NASB)

Some translations say "guard your heart." Either way, the meaning is clear: We are to pay attention to what's going on in our hearts. Why? Because, as the author suggests, each of us lives from the heart. And the health of your heart will be reflected in the quality of your life.

Like most kids, I was totally enthralled with what was going on around me, but I hadn't given a moment's thought to what was going on *inside* me. But this verse, along with my father's commentary, awakened me to the importance of monitoring what was rattling around in my heart.

Fast-forward twenty-five years. One night I was sitting on the edge of my son's bed, having one of those moments that every engaged parent lives for. We were talking about the events of the day.

Without thinking much about it, I put my hand on his chest and said, "Andrew, is everything okay in your heart?" As soon as I said it I thought, *Lighten up, Dad. He's eight. He doesn't have a clue what you are asking.*

But he paused, smiled, and said, "Yes, sir, Daddy."

That began a weekly, sometimes biweekly, habit that I have continued ever since. Andrew is thirteen now. He has heard me ask that question every week for five years. Since that time I have added a few other heart-related questions that I'll share with you later in this chapter.

THE VALUE OF A QUESTION

The questions you ask your children communicate to them what is important to you. The questions you repeatedly ask communicate what is *most* important to you in life.

How many times do you suppose your parents asked the following questions when you were growing up: "Did you brush your teeth?" "Did you do your homework?" "Did you finish your chores?" "Did you clean your room?" "How did you do on your test?" "Did you thank her?" "What time did you come in last night?" We knew from these questions what was important to our parents.

> Imagine how different your life might be if your parents had directed your attention to what was going on inside your heart.

After a while we knew what they were going to ask before they asked it. There was no point in asking if I could turn on the television on a school night if I hadn't done my homework. I knew that as soon as I asked about TV, my mom would ask about my homework. Anticipating my parents' questions shaped my behavior.

For most of us, the questions our parents asked revolved around our behavior, our performance. If you're like most adults, I bet you can't think of a single question your mom or dad repeatedly asked that caused you to stop and give thought to what was going on inside you. Consequently, we were never taught to pay attention to, much less guard, our hearts. We were taught, instead, to monitor our behavior. And there is certainly nothing wrong with that, except, as we have seen throughout this book, our hearts would eventually drive our behavior.

Imagine how different your life might be if your parents had instead directed your attention to what was going on inside your heart.

RETOOLING

I am convinced that one of the best ways to train our children to guard their hearts is through asking questions. Our questions have the power to do two things. First, they can communicate the value we place on the condition of their hearts. But more importantly, our questions can actually help our children know what they should be watching for. In time, our questions will become the gauge by which our children measure their hearts.

As I mentioned earlier, through the years I've added a few questions to my weekly bedtime routine with my children. One at a time I sit on the edge of their beds and ask my questions. They know them by heart.

"Is everything okay in your heart?"

"Are you mad at anybody?"

"Did anybody hurt your feelings today?"

"Did anybody break a promise to you today?"

"Is there anything you need to tell me?"

"Are you worried about anything?"

I ask about broken promises because I'm usually the culprit. If they think I've promised something and didn't follow through, I want them to talk about it, not sleep on it. I want my kids to learn how to clean out their hearts every day for the rest of their lives.

Recently, just to see how she would respond, I asked my nine-year-old daughter, "Whose failure would you secretly celebrate?" To be honest, I expected her to say, "What does that mean?" But her response shocked me. She immediately blurted out a name! Fortunately, it was not one of her brothers. But it was one of their friends.

I said, "Allie, do you even know what that question means?

She said, "Yes, sir. It means if they didn't do good at something, you would be glad about it."

As you might imagine, we had a nice little chat before she went to sleep that night. It turns out she had something lodged in her heart that we needed to get unlodged. I've since added that question to my repertoire.

DINNERTIME CONFESSION

The biggest payoff from all this heart talk came unexpectedly. As we were finishing dinner one night, I mentioned briefly that a friend of the family was sick again and that I thought his physical challenges were caused by "deeper" issues. Andrew latched right on to that.

"What deeper issues?" he asked.

This was someone they all knew, so I felt a little funny about continuing the conversation. But since I am always in search of a teach-able moment, I forged ahead anyway. For the next few minutes I explained the relationship between our physical health and the health of our hearts. I talked specifically about the danger of harboring secrets and how secrets can make you sick. Everybody seemed interested, so I kept going. I talked about how an incident in childhood could affect an adult later in life and how oftentimes the adult doesn't even remember the incident but is still affected. Then I made my application. "This is why it is so important to confess our sins. Confession keeps us from having unhealthy secrets stuck in our hearts."

I had barely gotten the last sentence out of my mouth when Garrett, who was nine at the time, said he needed to tell me something.

I said, "Okay."

He said, "Not here, Dad." Then he got up from the table and headed down the hall. I followed. When we were out of earshot from the rest of the family, Garrett proceeded to tell me about an incident that happened at a neighbor's house.

"When did this happen?" I asked.

"A long time ago," he replied.

I thanked him for telling me, hugged him, and told him how proud I was that he had emptied his heart. Then we went back to the dinner table.

Twenty minutes later, as Sandra and I were clearing the table, Garrett came into the kitchen and said, "Mom, can I talk to you for a minute?" She followed him down the hall and listened as he con-fessed the rest of the incident that he had only partially confessed to me. She hugged him and told him how proud she was of his desire to clean out his heart. Back in the kitchen, we both commented on how great it was that he was learning the importance of confession at such a young age. Little did we know…

At bedtime, that same night, Garrett asked if he could speak to Sandra alone. Once I left the room, he proceeded to confess another incident he had been feeling guilty about. This one was not quite as severe as the first.

An hour later, Sandra and I were working in our office and we heard the pitter-patter of little feet coming down the hall. It was Garrett. "I feel like I need to tell you guys something, but I don't know what it is." I told him to go back to bed and when it was clear to come back down and tell us.

A few minutes later he was back. "Dad," he said, "I remember what it was." I followed him back down the hall and listened as he told me about yet another incident that we didn't know about.

At ten-thirty Sandra and I were laying in bed, chuckling about Garrett's evening of confession, when once again we heard footsteps in the hall. It was Garrett. He came over to my side of the bed. It took everything in me not to say, "What else?" But I refrained.

"Mom, Dad," he said, "yesterday when Allie wasn't here I went into her room without asking." I knew we had finally reached the bottom of the confession barrel. He had scraped up every unconfessed sin he could come up with. Once again, I thanked him for his honesty. I assured him that God would honor his willingness to confess. Garrett peered at us through the dark and said, "I just don't want to get sick."

Now I know that sounds like a made-up preacher story, but that's just the way it happened. And I still haven't told you the best part. The next night, when we were saying our prayers with Garrett, he went through his normal prayer routine, but just before he said, "amen," he paused and added, "And thank you that I have a clean heart."

IMAGINE

What if we were all equally committed to scrubbing our hearts clean? Imagine what would happen if we made up our minds to never let the sun set on our anger, our greed, our jealousy, or our guilt. What if we guarded our hearts with the same diligence we use to guard our homes? And why not? After all, we know, we've seen, we've experienced what happens when a heart goes unattended. We have all felt the aftershock of anger, guilt, greed, and jealousy. We should wake up every day of our lives with an eye on the gauges of our hearts.

But better yet, imagine a generation of children who grow up attuned not only to what's happening around them but inside of them as well. Imagine your children growing up with an extraordinary sensitivity to the rhythms of their hearts. I don't have to tell you the difference that would make in their lives. You know the difference it would have made for you. Now you have an opportunity to do for your children what perhaps your parents did not know how to do for you.

As adults, we have been instructed to guard our hearts with all diligence. As parents, we have been given the responsibility to teach our kids to guard theirs. If the heart of your child is important to you, ask your child about what's going on in there. Teach your child to confess, forgive, give generously, and celebrate the successes of others. These are the habits that keep a heart free from painful clutter. These are habits that will enable your child to develop a healthy adult relationship with you in the future. These are the habits that change everything.

Chapter Nineteen

THE INVISIBLE MAN

Prof. Konrad: *Perhaps this is a civilization that exists without sex.*

Lt. Turner: *You call that civilization?*

Prof. Konrad: *Frankly, no.*

QUEEN OF OUTER SPACE (1958)

He that but looketh on a plate of ham and eggs to lust after it hath already committed breakfast with it in his heart.

C. S. LEWIS

No discussion of the heart would be complete without a word or two on the subject of lust. I imagine that a large percentage of my male readership would be happy to double their quotient of guilt, anger, greed, and jealousy if it meant they could be free of the lust that runs rampant in their hearts. If it were possible to arrange a four-for-one trade, a lot of men would make that trade in a heartbeat. And I'm sure there are a lot of wives who would be happy to broker the deal for their husbands.

At first glance, it may seem that lust is often to blame for at least three of the four heart disorders we have discussed. Sexual sin leads to guilt, for example. I've talked to dozens of people whose secrets stem from illicit sexual encounters, both invited and uninvited. And sexual sin always leads to anger. If your spouse has ever been unfaithful, you no doubt remember the rage you felt when you first discovered the betrayal. And lust can certainly fuel jealousy.

But there is another correlation between lust and our archenemies, guilt, anger, greed, and jealousy.

THERE IS A DIFFERENCE

First of all, lust is different from guilt, anger, greed, and jealousy in one very important way: God created it. He even declared it *good*. "So where's that verse?" you ask. Well, there's not really a verse that says as much, but it is certainly implied. When God created Adam and Eve, he also created the concept of *one flesh*. Every indication is that Adam strongly desired Eve, and Eve, Adam. With sex came lust. It was a package deal.

So lust can be a good thing. If it weren't for lust, you probably wouldn't have been born. Few of us would have gotten married. In a healthy marriage, lust is alive and well—and focused. Whereas guilt, greed, and jealousy are always signs of trouble, not so with lust. Lust can work for you or against you.

So before sin, there was lust. But as far as I can tell, greed, anger, guilt, and jealousy didn't show up until moments before the fall of mankind. Interestingly, all four were part of the story of our fall. And when sin entered the world, everything was corrupted. Including lust.

The other thing that's different about lust is that it's an appetite—it is not going away, no matter how spiritual or committed you are. Lust is not a problem you solve; it is an appetite that you manage. Thus the need for self-control. Lust can be focused but not eliminated. You can deal with your anger and guilt once and for all. But not lust. It is here for the duration. Well, it's here for a long time anyway.

IN SEARCH OF RESOLVE

Based on my conversations with hundreds of individuals whose misplaced lust has gotten them into trouble, I've drawn the following conclusion: Lust is rarely ever the root problem. When lust becomes problematic, it is almost always a manifestation of one or more of the heart problems we've already discussed. Clean out the anger, guilt, greed, and jealousy, and lust will become much more manageable. Deal with the big four, and your ability to exercise self-control in the arena of your sexuality will increase dramatically.

Anger and guilt, in particular, fuel sexual sin. Every man I've talked to who had a serious pornography addiction also had unresolved issues with his father. That's shrink-talk for "he's mad at his dad." Really mad! And as you might imagine, these men saw no correlation between their unresolved anger and their uncontrollable lust. But there is one: Pornography offers a substitute for intimacy—the very thing every man needs from his father.

Every woman I have talked to or heard about who was sexually promiscuous had secrets and hurts that dated back to childhood. Move past the issues normally associated with lust and you'll find a diseased heart—a heart lined with anger, guilt, and even jealousy.

Are there exceptions? I'm sure there must be, but I've never met or heard of one. Show me a man or woman who is battling lust on a larger-than-normal scale, and more than likely, I'll show you someone whose heart has been thoroughly invaded by one of the big four.

Simply put, guilt, anger, greed, and jealousy weaken our resolve against sexual temptation. In Paul's letter to the Christians in Ephesus, we get a glimpse into why this is the case. He writes, "'In your anger do not sin': Do not let the sun go down while you are still angry, and

Nothing destroys an individual's capacity for intimacy like sexual impurity.

do not give the devil a foothold." Clearly, Paul believed that unresolved anger gives the devil a base of operations in our lives. But a base to do what? Whatever he desires. The implication is clear: Deal with your anger and you take away the enemy's foothold; refuse to deal with it and you must prepare for the worst.

Unresolved anger serves as an avenue through which Satan can access any part of your life. And he is smart enough to know that nothing wreaks havoc on the human soul like sexual sin. Nothing destroys an individual's capacity for intimacy like sexual impurity. So he leverages our anger for his own ends, and in the end, we pay. Dearly.

Think about your own experience. Isn't it true that when you are angry you are more vulnerable to sexual temptation than normal? Anger distorts our thinking and thus our decision-making ability. Remember, when we are angry, it's because we are convinced that somebody owes us something. Anger desensitizes us to the harm we are inflicting on others or on ourselves—at a time when we feel we owe it to ourselves to do whatever we want.

Years ago, while working with high school students, I overheard a conversation I will never forget. I was driving a church van to camp, and two tenth-grade girls were seated directly behind me. At some point in their conversation one of the girls asked her friend, "Would you ever let Tim…" From there she described in teen-speech an activity considered by most as inappropriate for unmarried people to be involved in. But that wasn't the shocker. It was her friend's response that blew me away.

She said, "If I just had a fight with my mom, I might."

Say *what?* If she just had a fight with her mom? What did that have to do with anything? At fifteen years old, this young lady was already experiencing the relationship between her anger and her vulnerability sexually. Anger in one relationship made her vulnerable in another.

What's true of anger is also true of guilt, greed, and jealousy: All four reduce our resolve against sexual temptation. They tilt us off balance emotionally, leaving us vulnerable to lust. They're like out-of-control viruses weakening our spiritual immune system.

AN APPROPRIATE RESPONSE

So what do we do about lust? Ignore it? Chalk it up to a symptom that can't be helped? No. Lust must be contained. It must be properly focused. We will always have a need for self-control regardless of how healthy our hearts become. My point is simply this: Our battle for sexual purity must be waged on several fronts. But a healthy heart puts us in a stronger position to ward off temptation of all kinds. Confessing, forgiving, celebrating, and giving are habits that strengthen our resolve and remove the enemy's base of operation in our lives. The healthier our hearts, the easier it will be for us to keep this God-given appetite properly focused and under control.

Epilogue

BEGINNING OF THE END

Tony: *Scott, there may be side effects of this we don't know anything about.*

4D MAN (1959)

Klaatu: *I won't resort to threats, Mr. Harley. I merely tell you the future of your planet is at stake.*

THE DAY THE EARTH STOOD STILL (1951)

Perhaps it's good to have a beautiful mind,
  but an even greater gift is to have a beautiful heart.

JOHN NASH

onfess, forgive, give, celebrate. These are the habits that will change everything. Once these four routines define the rhythm of your heart, life will be noticeably different. Why? Because these habits empower you to settle your outstanding debts with others, God, and even yourself. Removing the debt-to-debtor dynamic from a relationship paves the way to better communication, understanding, and openness.

Confession allows us to come out from hiding. Forgiveness allows others to come out from under cover. Generosity allows us to partner with God as he shows himself in tangible ways to the world around us. Celebration makes us a vehicle through which God communicates his pleasure. That's what you were created for, and that's why these habits have the potential to change so much about our lives. Nothing goes untouched.

In case you haven't figured it out already, these four habits set us free to love as God intends for us to love. Anger, greed, guilt, and jealousy are the antithesis of love. As long as these four monsters grow unchecked in your heart, your efforts to love will be short-lived, thwarted. No amount of effort on your part can compensate. The purest of motives will not prevail. You cannot love while harboring one or more of these enemies—in the end, they will overcome.

To put this in perspective, consider these familiar verses from Paul's letter to the believers in Corinth:

> Love is patient, love is kind. It does not envy, it does not boast, it is not proud. It is not rude, it is not self-seeking, it is not easily angered, it keeps no record of wrongs. Love does not delight in evil but rejoices with the truth. It always protects, always trusts, always hopes, always perseveres. (1 Corinthians 13:4–7)

Angry people are not patient people. Guilty people are not kind. Jealous people are full of envy. Greedy people cannot help but boast. Anger makes us rude. Greed tempts us to be self-seeking. Jealousy thrives on scorekeeping. Greedy people are self-protecting. Guilt keeps us from trusting others because we have proved untrustworthy ourselves...

You get the point.

And yet we are *commanded* to love one another:

"A new command I give you: Love one another. As I have loved you, so you must love one another." (John 13:34)

Must. Jesus says we *must* love each other. And I'm sure you agree. But try embracing this command with a heart tainted by even one of the four fiends. Which means that until you deal with your anger, guilt, greed, and/or jealousy, you cannot obey the single most important command issued by our Lord.

Confess, forgive, give, celebrate. These four habits change everything because they free us to express and experience the most powerful force the human soul has ever encountered: unconditional love.

BEGINNING THE JOURNEY

Where do I go from here?

If you're not sure where to start, I can point you in the direction of someone who does know—the people who know you best, the people with whom you are doing life. Your husband. Your wife. Your children. Your parents. They catch the overflow of what's going on in your heart on a daily basis. They know exactly where you should start. Ask around. Here are a few conversation starters:

"Do you think I struggle with being completely open about things?"

"Do you feel like I have walls?"

"Do you ever feel like you're competing with my stuff?"

"Do you feel like I compare you to other women/men/children?"

"Are you ever afraid to talk to me?"

"Do you ever wonder which one of me you're going to come home to?"

Chances are, you already know how the people closest to you might answer some of these questions. If you decide to ask anyway, here's a suggestion. Decide ahead of time that you are not going to defend yourself. If you do, you won't learn a thing.

If you are not inclined to discuss this with your family and friends, then I recommend you go back to the section of this book that made you feel most uncomfortable. Odds are, that's where God would like to do something transformational in your life. Somewhere in the pages that made you wince and squirm and argue with me is a nugget or two of truth that your heavenly Father would like to gradually work deep into your soul.

Like a doctor whose skilled hands poke and probe until they find a sensitive spot, so God's truth has a way of finding its mark. But none of that can happen until you give God access to those sensitive, otherwise off-limits areas of your life. If you do, what may begin as a threatening and uncomfortable revelation may result in a freedom you never knew existed.

Narrator: *The end came swiftly. All over the world, their machines began to stop and fall. After all that men could do had failed, the Martians were destroyed and humanity was saved by the littlest things which God in his wisdom had put upon this Earth.*

War of the Worlds (1953)